"Ouch! That hurts. Truth does that, y... *Gods* is a book of hard truth. But it's e... writers are funny and authentic, write ...... do the self-righteousness thing. Truth also sets you free. This book will set you free. Maybe. Give it to everyone you know. They will either stone you or bless you. I rise up and call Ted and Kristin Kluck blessed!"

STEVE BROWN
Professor emeritus at Reformed Theological Seminary, and author and broadcaster with Key Life Network, Inc.

"This is Ted Kluck's best work to date. It is simultaneously personal, poignant, and brutally honest. But above all else it is undeniably challenging, both to the individual reader and—possibly even more important—to the institution of the church itself. Ted may not make many friends with this book, but I have no doubt that this book glorifies God."

REV. BENJAMIN J. ROBY
Senior pastor of Heritage Baptist Church, Ashland, OH, and Bible instructor at Veritas Classical Christian Academy, Ashland, OH

"Employing tales and terms that are both humorous as well as humbling, Kristin and Ted Kluck unmask the domestic gods of our age. Rather than simply marveling at how easily we bend the knee before idols such as sports and cynicism, the Klucks offer clear and compelling correctives that are seated in Scripture. Gen Xers and Millennials will especially resonate with the Klucks' style, but this is a transgenerational primer addressing the challenges of our age in the light of God's Word."

RANDALL J. GRUENDYKE, DMin
Campus pastor at Taylor University and contributor to *Preach the Word: Essays on Expository Preaching: In Honor of R. Kent Hughes*

"The ancient Israelites persecuted God's prophets because the Israelites loved their idols so much and because their idols were so ingrained in their culture. We read these texts and feel self-righteous because we don't bow down to little statues; meanwhile our lives our chock-full of things we put above Jesus. Thank God for the honesty of His prophets, and thank God for the honesty of the Klucks' voice, helping us all keep Jesus as the center of our lives!"

NOAH FILIPIAK
Founding pastor of Crossroads Church, Lansing, MI, and author of www.AtACrossRoads.net

"Imagine a reality entertainer who shows off what embarrasses him, not what titillates you. Imagine a searing critique of evangelical culture by a prophet who indicts himself. Imagine an inspirational story where a loser doesn't make a comeback, but he does meet Jesus Christ. Actually, don't imagine it; read this book."

CORY HARTMAN
Pastor, First Baptist Church of Hollidaysburg, PA

"In *Household Gods*, Ted and Kristin Kluck speak openly and honestly about the idols Christians encounter within their own homes. With humility and humor, they point the reader to sins of the heart and to the Savior who is greater than those sins."

STEPHEN ALTROGGE
Author of *The Greener Grass Conspiracy* and *Untamable God*

"*Household Gods* might best be described as a comedic devotional. Anyway, that's the best I can do at categorizing a book that is at once so funny and spiritually enriching. Ted Kluck—with help from his wife, Kristin—lays bare not only his own heart but the reader's as well, for we all nurture our own family idols. And along the way we are treated to vintage Kluckian cultural commentary, regarding everything from youth sports leagues to the Christian publishing industry. You will laugh with conviction."

JAMES S. SPIEGEL
Taylor University

"As an author, when I read Ted Kluck I feel a bit like a garage-band guitar hero who gets a front-row ticket to see Clapton. He starts the concert, hunkered in his seat, eyes locked on the fingerings, intent on stealing his riffs . . . until he gets caught up in the music and rises to his feet. Ted's unique voice—modern, postmodern, edgy, and efficient—draws me in every time. This has never been truer than in this book about love and legalism, values and expectations, parenting and pedestals. Ted and Kristin have written a book that takes biblical concepts from the lips of the prophets and the pens of the apostles and translates them into our world of little league, Wes Anderson movies, alumni magazines, and grinding concrete. The result is challenging, uplifting, and freeing."

ZACHARY BARTELS
Author of *Playing Saint*

"Ted and Kristin's collaboratively written book, *Household Gods*, gives the reader a candid look at the various idols that distract families from focusing on the truly important things in life. Their narrative is relatable and provides helpful lessons to learn. Instead of living vicariously through their sons or with a self-absorbed focus on family success, the Klucks describe a family relationship that better reflects a communion with our Lord. I look forward to learning the valuable lessons shared by Ted and Kristin and incorporating them into my family."

NATHAN LEAMER

household
gods

FREED FROM THE WORSHIP OF FAMILY
TO DELIGHT IN THE GLORY OF GOD

TED *and* KRISTIN KLUCK

NAVPRESS

A NavPress resource published in alliance
with Tyndale House Publishers, Inc.

NAVPRESS⬤®

NavPress is the publishing ministry of The Navigators, an international Christian organization and leader in personal spiritual development. NavPress is committed to helping people grow spiritually and enjoy lives of meaning and hope through personal and group resources that are biblically rooted, culturally relevant, and highly practical.

For more information, visit www.NavPress.com.

A NavPress resource published in alliance with Tyndale House Publishers, Inc.

NAVPRESS and the NAVPRESS logo are registered trademarks of NavPress, The Navigators. Absence of ® in connection with marks of NavPress or other parties does not indicate an absence of registration of those marks.

TYNDALE is a registered trademark of Tyndale House Publishers, Inc.

ISBN 978-1-61291-585-2

Cover design by Faceout Studio, Tim Green

Interior design by Dean H. Renninger

Cover photograph of car copyright © Michael Bodmann/Getty Images. All rights reserved.

Cover photograph of warning sign copyright © StockSolutions/Thinkstock. All rights reserved.

Published in association with the literary agency of Wolgemuth & Associates, Inc.

Library of Congress Cataloging-in-Publication Data

Kluck, Ted.
Household gods : freed from the worship of family to delight in the glory of God / Ted and Kristin Kluck.
     pages cm
  Includes bibliographical references.
  ISBN 978-1-61291-585-2
1. Families—Religious aspects—Christianity. 2. Families—Religious
life. 3. Idolatry. 4. Spiritual warfare. I. Title.
  BT707.7.K58 2014
  261.8'3585—dc23   2014023491

Printed in the United States of America

19	18	17	16	15	14
6	5	4	3	2	1

Oh dear Dad, can you see me now?

I am myself, like you somehow.

PEARL JAM, "RELEASE"

Contents

Foreword

The household is becoming a dangerous place.

Or maybe it's always been that way.

For all the outrage from both the church and conservative media that the family is being attacked, hijacked, undervalued, and redefined, it seems that little weight is ever given to the thought that one of the biggest threats to families may actually come from the inside.

It's a subtle thing. In our desire to bring family values back to the forefront of our culture, could it be possible that we've over-corrected and created an impenetrable idol out of them instead? Did God really intend for our families to be the one thing we can never spend too much time, energy, love, and money on? Or have we proudly turned our households into golden calves that we dutifully serve as they subtly enslave our hearts?

Although the evangelical church has much to say about a society that makes gods out of careers, sports, hobbies, and cash money, the home will rarely if ever get added to the list of things for us to be on guard against. In fact, just the opposite seems to be true.

We applaud the dad who obsessively devotes all of his time, energy, and attention to his spouse, kids, and house. We admire the mom who tirelessly commits her life to soccer games, dance recitals, playdates, and school activities. It's admirable. Selfless. Sacrificial. It's what *good* parents do. It's what *other* parents who aren't doing them aspire to do.

The reality is that few people are ever going to call out anyone for finding their identity in hearth and home because we don't believe it's actually possible to do that, do we? After all, our first ministry is to our family, isn't it? The problem couldn't possibly be that we're giving *too much* attention to domesticity, could it? Unfortunately, in a world that appears to be at war trying to redefine what marriage and the traditional family are supposed to look like, evangelicals and conservatives alike may be creating an equally damaging alternative: the deification of it.

So how do we guard our hearts from worshipping at the altar of family and finding our identity from the household gods of this age? What did God actually intend for our families to be for both us and Him?

Ted and Kristin take us on an honest and courageous journey chronicling how the life of their household became the god of their lives. You'll read stories of how good gifts from God cease to be blessings when they draw our hearts away from our good God. And like all great stories, you'll shed some tears over the loss they suffered and share the joy they experienced as God led them down the road to restoration and relationship.

Ronnie Martin, church planter and coauthor of
Finding God in the Dark

Acknowledgments

The biggest and most heartfelt note of thanks goes to our dear friends Jean-Mi and Dominique Hosdez, of Andel, France, where we wrote parts of this book. In addition to being the owner and president of the St. Brieuc Licornes American Football Club, Jean-Mi was our de facto translator, arranger of vehicles, tour guide, sommelier, gourmand, and best friend. And Dominique has become a dear friend, a sister, really, to Kristin. We love and miss you and your beautiful family so much. A special shout-out to Lena and Jade from Tristan and Maxim, as well.

To Pac, Clem, Max, Arnaud, Ray, Taz, Mike, Mathieu, Momo, Jann, Dominic, Jean-Marc, Kenny, Tomas, both Kevins, and the rest of St. Brieuc Licornes: Thank you for accepting me, listening to my English, going to battle with me in Caen after only three days, and becoming my friends. You guys are an amazing group of computer programmers, dentists, truck drivers, office workers, and football players. You defy American football stereotypes in every way. Never stop loving and taking care of each other. You're a great team, regardless of what the scoreboard says.

Special thanks as well to the high schools in Lamballe and St. Brieuc, where I taught flag football—especially to Gilles Commeault of Lycee-Renan and his wife, Valerie Commeault of Lycee-St. Marie. You're lovely people!

Thank you to Pastor Michael Piette and his family, and to the Evangelical Church of St. Brieuc for welcoming us for six weeks, faithfully preaching the Word, and providing translation.

And thank you to Thierry Boisrame for the lovely accommodations at Au Clos Du Lit in St. Aaron, where we woke up to a rooster crowing and unspeakable beauty each morning. Sorry we were always using the washing machine and your Internet connection.

And a general but heartfelt thank-you to everyone in France who extended kindness to us during our stay. We never experienced the stereotypical uptight, judgmental, and American-disdaining French. Instead, we were met with curiosity, smiles, helpfulness, and kindness every step of the way. Thank you.

Stateside, a big thank you to Auntie for the airport runs (and the new battery and alternator), to Derek and Mallory for taking care of the mail (which was a *big* concern for some people), and to Bruce for blowing the snow during the annual winter apocalypse that hits our area and which we were happy to miss this year.

Thank you to Don, Brian, Liz, and the rest of the team

at NavPress, and to Andrew Wolgemuth for being the best agent in the business. In particular to Liz Heaney, our editor, who did something during the course of our process that was as yet unprecedented for me in almost a decade in this business: apologizing for something. It's not important (to the reader) what it was, just that it happened. That was a huge encouragement to me and proof that God is real and that He works on our hearts in tangible and amazing ways.

Thank you, Cory Hartman, for getting me through the editing process as you always do. For listening, for gently pushing back if need be, and for just understanding.

We're grateful for Norm, Phil, their families, and the rest of the leadership at Covenant Life Community Church in East Lansing, where families are loved but not idolized.

Finally, to our own families, both nuclear[1] and extended. We love you very much. Thank you for your love, patience, and forgiveness with us. You're not perfect, and neither are we, but you already knew that.

A Note from Ted

I always do this. I always end up writing two introductions. I write the first one right at the beginning—usually at the book proposal stage, before the whole thing has even been *consummated* by a contract—and then the second one, this one, at the end.

What I've always wanted from people in my family, maybe more than anything, are collections of stories. I wish my dead grandparents had written down all their stories. Same with great-uncles and great-aunts. Same with my parents. I think more than anything I just want to know about their lives. I want to know everything—from the mundane to the heroic to the grotesque and shameful. Of course, nobody does this; nobody writes everything down. However, it's what I've tried to do with all my books—even the teachy ones (like this one)—so that when I'm dead and gone, my kids and grandkids will at least know what I was up to all these years. Maybe they'll have a shot at not making the same mistakes I've made. Maybe they'll have a better shot at loving the Lord and loving their neighbor.

I teach a university class called Mass Media Literacy. Nobody really knows what the class is supposed to accomplish, and as such, we often end up talking about movies we like (such is the beauty of the communications major). One morning, after delving deeply into the work of filmmaker Wes Anderson, it occurred to me that all of his films are about family.

And what's more, all of Anderson's films are about the sins that "present" in family contexts: greed[1], pride[2], arrogance[3], selfishness[4], sibling rivalry[5], sports[6], celebrity[7], lust[8], adultery[9], and so on. One of my students made the incredibly insightful comment that "In Wes Anderson movies, adults act like children and children act like adults." I'm always jealous of the Bill Murray character, who gets to sulk and be disenfranchised for the duration of each of these films; however, when I try to sulk and be disenfranchised in my own family, it doesn't come off nearly as charming.

The fact that I like these movies so much is probably part of the reason I'm often so bad at living in a family and loving them as I should. That, and my sin nature.

Like a Wes movie, this book is part didactic and part storytelling. Though the book is "about" family idolatry in a broad sense, many of the chapters are about specific idolatries that present, or show themselves, in a family context. You may be tempted to wonder, *What does this chapter have to do with family idolatry?* Think, rather, *How might this idolatry manifest itself in a family context?*

Not that I'm telling you what to think.

Because we live in a time and place where Christians sometimes seem to love fighting about issues almost as much as they love the Lord, here's a short list of issues that we *won't* be fighting about in this book, partly because the Bible isn't explicit (or really even implicit) about them, and also because we don't feel called to write about them. Search your own heart as to whether you're making idols of these family-related concerns:

- how many children to have
- whether you should homeschool your children or send them to public school

The things you'll read in this book are all things we've struggled with, or are currently struggling with. Kristin and I bring them to you humbly, in hopes that they will challenge and encourage you, and bring glory to our Lord.

Family Idolatry and Other Household Gods

You shall have no other gods before me.
— EXODUS 20:3

If you lined up, side by side, every printed, photographic evangelical Christmas card, they would wrap around the globe three times. You know the cards I'm referring to. In the South, the Beautiful Family is all adorned in the same khaki pants, blue dress shirts, and yellow ties. Dresses for the ladies. Up north, it's a bit more casual, and by casual I mean everyone is wearing matching jeans and fashionable white T-shirts or matching North Face jackets if the photo was taken in the cold. Sometimes the family dog is included.[1]

If you lined up all these cards side by side, it would be mile after glorious mile of nice-looking, affluent, well-groomed, perfect-seeming families. Miles and miles of mountain scenes in the background (from our ski trip!) or ocean vistas in the background (we live in North Carolina!) or poor people in the background (we're missionaries and we have big hearts if not a lot of money!). Miles and miles of less-than-engaging copy about how hubby's job is awesome, the kids are all getting straight As, Mom is *so busy* (but handling it well), and about the new bambino on the way (What a surprise! How will we deal with it?). The khaki pants alone would cover most of Europe and Asia. The accompanying letters would cover South America. The family dogs would cover Central America.

There's seemingly no end to how impressed we are with our own families, and how badly we want you to know about it.

As a group we book-purchasing evangelicals are, for the most part, a well-educated, affluent, and decent-looking lot. We clean up and photograph well. Our kids do well in school. And if we don't have all the money in the world then, hey, at least we have our Great Families, right? Well, not exactly.

The two of us grew up believing, albeit subconsciously, that being a good, successful Christian involves having a good, successful family. (Sound familiar, anyone?) Here are some of the lies we told ourselves:

- If I'm single, having a husband or wife will fulfill me and make life great.
- If I'm childless, having a child will fulfill me and make life great.
- If God loves me, He'll bless me with a family whose job it is to provide me with a nonstop cavalcade of Kodak moments and splendid memories.

In our experience many churches continue, year after year, to subconsciously sell these lies to their congregations. The stuff of our family fantasies includes an adoring, faithful spouse; attractive, obedient kids; people who depend on us, love us, give us a reason to get out of bed, and regularly stand up and sing our praises.

Many of us worship at the altar of The Perfect Family. It's worship at the altar of family that causes the mom in your women's Bible study to post the sixty-seventh photo of her daughter's birthday party on Facebook. It causes Dad to spend an additional thirty hours a week playing football with his son so his kid can get a college football scholarship. It's the reason for the magazine-quality family photos all over the house. Family is a prominent household god.

IDOLATRY DEFINED

All this talk of household gods can be confusing. How can something good (family, professional success, comfort) be something bad (an idol)?

In his great book *Counterfeit Gods*, author Timothy Keller defines an idol as "anything more important to you than God, anything that absorbs your heart and your imagination more than God, anything you seek to give you what only God can give."[2] Our wise friend and counselor, Pat, has explained it to me this way: Anything we feel like we have a "right" to have is an idol (a loving spouse, healthy kids, sufficient income, a nice house, a good-paying job). Anything we feel we can't be happy without is an idol (more of the same). Anything that, if lost, would cause utter despair (not sorrow, not pain, but despair—a sense that all is lost, God is cruel, you want to die).

Keller writes that "the human heart takes good things like a successful career, love, material possessions, and even family, and turns them into ultimate things. Our hearts deify them as the center of our lives because, we think, they can give us significance and security, safety and fulfillment, if we attain them."[3]

We look to our household gods to give us "significance and security, safety and fulfillment." We elevate and worship them when they succeed at making us feel this way. When they don't, we feel devastated and personally affronted or shafted by God, as though The Perfect Family, The Perfect Job, The Perfect House, and so on were our birthright as Christians. And when I say "we" I mean "I."

Of all the household gods, family idolatry is the most tricky to identify because of the value the Bible places on family. The family is the building block of a moral society. It is a hedge of protection for the vulnerable children and women of that society. The Bible talks a lot about what a blessing a godly spouse[4] and a house full of children[5] are, and it has a lot of directives on how to keep those relationships healthy and godly.[6] Parents are charged with the precious task of directing and guiding our children's hearts toward God, so it is easy to think of family as an unqualified good. "Family values" is practically synonymous with "Orthodox Christian."

Family is a good gift from God, and we are right to love, cherish, and protect it from harm. We are right to grieve when we lose a family member, when we see a disabled child who cannot fully experience life, or when we experience a broken relationship. These tragedies are all evidence of sin in our world, and it is right to grieve them and to rage against the sin that has marred God's beautiful creation. But at some point, even without realizing it, we can cross a line with our love and cherishing and protecting. We cross the line into idolatry when we begin to love the gifts God has given us more than we love Him. When we rage at Him and question Him if things go wrong in our families. Idolatry is a matter of the heart.

WHY THIS BOOK?

Writing a book about household gods is tough, because in order to be good, it *has* to be honest. In order to have a shot at being interesting, it has to be honest. I think, personally, in order to be a Christian book about idolatry and family, it has to be honest. There are droves of family books, some of them even good, that say all the right things and make the author look like a big sweetie. I could write a book about "dating my wife" or raising a little Christian knight that would make me look like a real swell husband or a real amazing dad. Probably all of my male readers would roll their eyes and secretly hate me. I wouldn't blame them. I've secretly hated Christian authors like that for years.

If this introduction introduces nothing else, let it introduce this: I'm not that author (nor is Kristin). I'm a sinner in specific and hurtful ways, and I'm sometimes a jerk to my family. On these pages I've written about the different household gods we've worshipped—not as a means of glorifying our sinfulness, but as a means of exposing it and thanking God for His grace and sanctifying work. Before nearly every book I tell Kristin, "This is probably going to be my last book," because I'm convinced that people will hate it and I'll never get another opportunity to write. I'm sure some people will hate this one because it exposes and challenges some idols that many of us hold dear.

Still, the idea of discovering, naming, and outing new sins seems to be a particular passion in the particular sub-subculture (Young Reformeddom) that I'm in. We like the idea of being tough on sin and, as such, have made it our goal to discover and name new sins in the same way that astronomers used to discover and name new stars.[7] I hope and pray that this won't be "that" kind of book. I hope that we can teach through our stories, come alongside you in your struggles, and reach for the Cross together.

In the midst of a Christian subculture that idolizes the family, an evangelical history that overcelebrated it, and a secular culture that overprograms it, it is easy for well-meaning Christians to cross over the line into family idolatry. Kristin and I know, because that has certainly been the case for us. This book isn't meant to judge. It isn't written to crack wise about the latest evangelical trends. We want to share with you the idols that have been exposed in our lives with the hope of helping you identify some of you own.

We will examine the culture that spawned family idolatry and also share with you the steps we have taken to adjust our perspective, flee this and other household gods, and escape to the Cross. The first few chapters will focus specifically on family idolatry, and then we will move on to talk about household gods that arise within the context of family.

A word about how this book is structured: I write the majority of the material, and Kristin chimes in whenever she has something to say. Her stuff is in a different font and preceded by her name. We didn't feel the need or compulsion to shoehorn her into every chapter because that (formulaity, shoehorning, and so on) is part of what's wrong with this industry, in our humble (or, more accurately, not-so-humble) opinions.

This book is for friends, for family, and for us. For people who search for their identities on Little League fields, or who feel like they're failing, silently, in church pews. This is a book for anyone who's ever looked at the day-to-day life of their family, felt it's out of control—felt that priorities and focuses weren't quite right—and wanted to change, but didn't know how. It's for people who love their family, but perhaps have elevated that love higher than it should be. It's for anyone who feels like all they do is compete—at sports, at academics, and at the arts. And it's a book for those who are interested in reclaiming the humble joy of and proper perspective on life, particularly when it comes to family.

Matthew 5:4 reads, "Blessed are those who mourn." Kristin and I mourn and grieve our sins. We have struggled—and still struggle—with many of these household gods. We write this book from a fundamental position of poverty of spirit (Matthew 5:3). We invite you to be impoverished with us, and then invite you to gaze at our Redeemer by repenting and feeling God's mercy.

CHAPTER 1

Spawning Family Idolatry

It is difficult to question anyone who explains that he wants a certain position of authority because God plans to use him in it (which is why this problem is so difficult to deal with).

— CHERYL FORBES, *THE RELIGION OF POWER*

"Everybody in our church growing up had a big family . . . usually seven to ten kids . . . always homeschooled . . . and there was the pressure that all of those kids would be perfect and that, as a family, we'd all have some skill like singing together or drama," explains my friend about growing up in what sounds like a strange, burlap-jumpsuited, evangelical re-creation of *The Brady Bunch, The Partridge Family,* and *The Sound of Music.*

My friend is in his early thirties. Married. A father of two. An avid pickup basketball player. An excellent public school

English teacher. A lover of books, Scripture, and the gospel. All of that to say he's remarkably, or perhaps unremarkably, normal. We invited his wife and him over because they are, to our knowledge, the only other couple in our church who aren't homeschooling. That makes them, potentially, prime friend material, being that homeschooling is the tie that binds people socially in our church.

"We didn't watch television, didn't watch movies, and couldn't listen to music with drums. We didn't date, we courted, which of course makes it more spiritual and of course makes it better," he says with a chuckle. It's the kind of chuckle that acknowledges the weirdness, but in a nonbitter way. "In our cult[1] it was normal to be disdainful and wary of things like the government, college, and especially women who had jobs outside the home. It was normal to want to grow your own food, make your own clothes, and be 'self-sustaining.'"

What he's describing is a version of Christian life in which the Christian family is, ideally, sequestered or cut off from the culture at large and is a self-sustaining, apprenticeship-generating, college-disdaining, government-distrusting unit. It's a version of family that takes seriously the verse that says "be fruitful, and multiply"[2] but often seems to disregard Scriptures on being salt and light in the world and not hiding your light under a bushel.[3]

At some point over pizza it occurs to us that what my friend has been describing sounds eerily familiar to the de facto dominant subculture in conservative evangelicalism, at least in the Midwest, where we are. The disdain for government, the emphasis on family, and the "circling the wagons" mentality are all points of overlap.

"That sounds like what's popular now," I say, to no one in particular.

In *The Pursuit of God* A.W. Tozer wrote, "We imitate each other with slavish devotion. Our most strenuous efforts are put forth to try to say the same thing that everyone around us is saying—and yet to find an excuse for saying it, some little variation on the approved theme or, if no more, at least a new illustration."[4] Tozer could have been writing in direct, critical response to today's evangelical blogosphere or church culture, except that he penned that particular sentence around 1948, proving at some level that there is nothing new under the sun.

Wrote Janet Fishburn in 1991's *Confronting the Idolatry of Family:*

> *A mother knew she was a success if her children followed the prescribed pattern. Her crowning achievement was visible whenever the family was together again—at worship in the "family pew." Though parents might have been unhappy knowing that some of the younger generation were there under duress, it did not matter a great deal. The important thing was that they were there.*[5]

This definitely squares with Kristin's description of her upbringing, which was in many ways easy and idyllic, as her parents were on staff with one of the 1980s prominent family ministries in evangelicalism. Being, though, that their family was essentially her parents' "product," Kristin felt a great deal of pressure when she was trotted out in front of supporting churches on the family's annual summer support-gathering tours.[6] In her teenage years, grappling with questions of the faith seemed to take a distant backseat to looking right and saying the right things in front of people who mattered (read: supporters). This bothered her, and still does.

LEGALISM'S APPEAL

Why is slipping into law-based Christianity, fakery, and group-think appealing to so many? Especially in a family context?

It's appealing because legalism makes following Christ easy, because it takes critical thinking and discernment out of the equation. Instead of studying Scripture, seeking God for comfort and counsel, and listening to the Holy Spirit in the midst of life's struggles, we can look to religious leaders for the answers. For example, Bill Gothard sold the dream of having an "ATI" family, which is about as eighties and corporate as it sounds. ATI stands for "Advanced Training Institute"—it provides training seminars for doctors, lawyers, teens, and families and includes life training on everything from what kind of a girl to marry to how to buy makeup to how to stand around as a guy when you're, well, standing around (seriously).[7] No area of life has gone uncommented upon by Gothard's company.

It's this—the commenting upon of certain areas of life that fall outside of biblical directives (example: Paul didn't write another letter to the Ephesians telling them how to tuck in their shirts or how to stand around[8])—that resulted in the rampant legalism that ruined lots of kids' Christian school experiences in the eighties and homeschool experiences in the nineties, after God's explicit plan for education became homeschooling and not Christian schooling.

My friend, by the grace of God, has ended up remarkably normal and cool.

THE PROBLEM OF SIN

It's worth noting that we can't blame our family of origin, or Bill Gothard, or even trendiness for family idolatry. While Kristin and I somehow latched on to the 1990s ethic of "if something is really popular it must be bad,"[9] we recognize that family idolatry didn't start in the 1980s and certainly not with Gothard. And it's not finding its apex in today's large-family-homeschool-dominant culture. So the problem isn't cultural trends. The problem is sin, and the problem is me.

Paul wrote in Romans 3 that "Jews and Gentiles alike are all under the power of sin,"[10] and that "there is no one righteous, not even one,"[11] and later "for all have sinned and fall short of the glory of God."[12] The problem is that, although I mean well, my motives are inherently flawed. I want my kids to make me look great. I want all of my decisions about family size and schooling to turn out great so that I look good.

I need God's help to recognize these idolatries, confess them, and fight them. Paul captured this with brutal clarity in Romans 7:24-25, when he wrote, "What a wretched man I am! Who will rescue me from this body that is subject to death? Thanks be to God, who delivers me through Jesus Christ our Lord!"

EVERYWHERE PRESENT

To be fair, family idolatry is not solely an evangelical problem. We see it in our own fairly average suburb. We see it every time we go to a ball game or performing arts event that our kids are involved in. We see it every time we spot a fifth grader's name and number emblazoned on the back of his mother's sweatshirt[13] in the stands of a peewee football game. We see it in every harried family taking different cars in different directions to different sports practices only to reconnect at the end of the night to collapse into bed. We see it in our own hearts when we're disappointed that *our* child may not be the star.

We see it in the financial product advertisements that suggest that if we aren't building a financial fortress for our children and grandchildren, we're not doing right by them. We see it in the ads that suggest that if I don't buy my wife the hearts-on-fire pendant or tennis bracelet, I may not get the warm, suggestive television embrace that must mean that she really does love me.

We see it in the commercials that suggest that if we *really* love our children we'd buy the car with the extra air bags, or we'd start saving for college, or we'd take them to Disneyland where we could engineer a childhood's worth of family memories for the cost of airfare and a hotel suite.

I'm saying that—Christian and secular—we're all in danger of getting the value of family horribly wrong. So how do we stem the tide? How do we protect our hearts from something that, on the surface, seems so good, and is even celebrated and subtly encouraged?

It starts with searching our own hearts and our own motives, and with a healthy recognition of who we are without Christ, which is to say that we are "dead in [our] transgressions and sins."[14] Even if we look good and have reasonably well-behaved kids, we're still dead in our sins apart from Christ. It starts with a call to think more deeply about the things we want and why we want them. It starts with a willingness to indict ourselves, which can be one of the hardest things in the world to do.

⇝ *From Kristin* ⇜

Imagine the kind of women's Bible study/gab session/hen party that happens all across the country. Imagine a little urn of coffee in the corner. Imagine danishes. Imagine name tags. Imagine a full-to-bursting lactation room around the corner. Imagine that the leader of said study asks, as she always does, "Tell us a little about yourselves!"

Gag. Cue family idolatry. As the dreaded Infertile Woman, I hate this part of these studies the most. The part where the woman in the fashionable jeans and faux-hippie dress exclaims, "I have five beautiful, healthy kids and I'm so blessed!" The part where the woman in the college hoodie says, "I've been married to my husband for ten years, and he's my knight in shining armor." The part where the overly enthusiastic leader then claps, middle-school-cheerleader-style (fingertips up and together), and says, "Yay!"

This is the part where I deflate and wonder how I'm going to deal with my own family-idolatry issues. This is where I wonder if I'm the problem, or if our culture is the problem. This is the part where I want to run away.

CHAPTER 2

Love Will Tear You Apart

THE HOUSEHOLD GOD OF BEING SOMEONE'S IDOL

I long for the days of disorder. I want them back, the days when I was alive on the earth, rippling in the quick of my skin, heedless and real. I was dumb-muscled and angry and real.
— *UNDERWORLD* BY DON DELILLO

Where have all the cowboys gone?
— PAULA COLE

Forgive me for referencing an antiquated 1990s Paula Cole song in the epigraphs, because, let's face it, Paula Cole was never cool even when she was cool. But I thought it was appropriate. I'm not single, obviously. But Kristin and I have lots of friends who are, and frankly, I couldn't help but notice, partly by observation and partly by them telling me, how hard it can be for singles in our churches.

Our female single friends say things like, "There are no

single guys at church," and even our single guy friends say things like, "There are no other single guys to hang out with." They're right. Now, by way of caveat, this may not be an "everywhere" problem. But here in the Midwest, Christians seem to love (a) getting married really young, and (b) cranking out a bunch of kids. These things, officially[1] and unofficially,[2] are celebrated in our churches. Which is a good thing—unless you are one of the few people who don't fit into that square peg, and then you just feel like you don't belong at church. You feel that you don't count as a person until you're part of a couple. This is a bit of a problem for singles everywhere, but shouldn't it be different in church?

"There has never been a very secure place for single adults in 'the family pew,'" wrote Janet Fishburn in *Confronting the Idolatry of Family*. "There is the sense that 'something is wrong' with adults who do not marry."[3] I think we sometimes conveniently forget that Scripture addresses singleness, and even at times encourages it. First Corinthians 7 reads, "I would like you to be free from concern. An unmarried man is concerned about the Lord's affairs—how he can please the Lord. But a married man is concerned about the affairs of this world—how he can please his wife—and his interests are divided."[4] Paul certainly isn't demanding that everyone be single, but at the same time he makes a compelling case for remaining unmarried.

What I think is great about these single friends of ours is that they love their churches. They love the robust, biblical preaching, and they even love all the married people and huge families, which is convenient because they're surrounded by both. They've put up graciously with being the only single in our married-people small groups and being photographed alone for the church directory, and they don't hold it against us when we call them to babysit, even though they're thirty and hold advanced degrees and have successful careers. Let's face it: being single is a different place in life than being married, with different needs, responsibilities, schedules, finances, and time available.

What our single friends don't love is that in order to embrace things such as robust doctrine, they're missing out on meeting other Christian people who are youngish and single and may go to bigger, more megachurchy, meat-markety singles' groups. Single women want to be plugged in and valued as individuals, not just as potential halves of future couples. Consequently, many are spending years waiting for their ethereal Perfect Life Partner to show up.[5] What too many singles don't realize is that he or she will never show up, whether or not they ever marry.

THE BEGINNING OF OUR IDOLATRY

Every great American movie is a love story, and love stories all end with couples who get together. *Say Anything*, the greatest romantic comedy of all time starring the King of the Romantic Comedy, John Cusack, is the story of Lloyd Dobler, a character so earnest, kind, selfless, and single-minded in his devotion that he could have only been the creation of a writer intent on creating a male character so perfect that the rest of us would have no chance of keeping up.

In the great Will Ferrell dramedy *Stranger Than Fiction*, Harold Crick, played by Ferrell, visits Dr. Jules Hilbert, a literature professor portrayed brilliantly by Dustin Hoffman, to find out if he's living in a comedy or tragedy. "In a tragedy at the end you die," explains Dr. Hilbert.[6] "In a comedy you get hitched."

Kristin's and my love story began in the Taylor University cafeteria sometime in the spring of 1996. As a private Christian college, it naturally attracts many students from affluent families. I thought of them as North-Facey rich kids from the suburbs of Grand Rapids. Being from a small, depressing blue-collar town down the road didn't fill me with confidence in the romance department. I figured Taylor girls wanted guys who drove Lexuses and played soccer, not football players who drove old GMC pickups.

Make that ex-football players. I had just broken the same leg twice, and gone through an operation and a failed comeback in fall camp. Being that it was the mid-1990s, I was rocking a look that fell somewhere on the spectrum between former Oklahoma linebacker Brian Bosworth and Soundgarden guitarist Jerry Cantrell. I was comfortable being moody, sullen, and quiet, as this sort of fit the grunge ethos, and with my having lost an idol (football) and having not yet found anything that could come even close to replacing it.

Enter Kristin. A senior. A theater girl. Being that it was the mid-1990s, she wore cable-knit grunge sweaters, cutoff shorts over tights, and work boots. If you came of age in this era, I don't have to explain how hot this was. In a Christian college setting where marriage was unabashedly worshipped and celebrated as the pinnacle of female existence, she was sweating her impending graduation. As a young Christian college girl, graduating without a husband, a fiancé, or at the least a boyfriend meant that you had invested tens of thousands of dollars and had nothing to show for it but a degree (though nobody would ever verbalize this). To say that there was a good bit of hand-wringing among singles in female senior housing would be a massive understatement, because when can a Christian girl ever again expect to be in the presence of several hundred well-heeled, well-educated, guitar-under-a-tree-playing, mission-trip-taking Christian guys?

I was eating dinner by myself one night. This, at Taylor, you did not do. But being the Grunge Bosworth that I was, I flouted convention and did whatever I wanted in hopes that somebody would notice me doing whatever I wanted and think it was cool enough to want to talk to me. Kristin noticed. She began by flirting with me about my hair, which was, all false-humility aside, nineties-awesome in that it was long in front and shaved in the back/sides. Finally, that night, she came and sat at my table. I spotted her out of the corner of my eye having dinner with another guy whom she left in order to come and sit with me. This was perhaps my first taste of being idolized/adored by a woman, and I liked it.

She sat down and we talked for hours before the staff cinematically began closing down the cafeteria around us.

"I have a very important question to ask you," Kristin said. By this time I was hooked. Eye contact was constant. Heart rate elevated. I was ready to change my major, forget about football, and follow this girl to the ends of the earth. "Ask me anything," I replied.

"How do you feel about girls asking guys out?" she said. Being that this was still the mid-1990s and *I Kissed Dating Goodbye* hadn't yet been written, I thought I had just hit the lottery. I didn't know that I should have given her a senatorial filibuster about the potential pitfalls of quote/unquote dating and how the guy should initiate and how our families should be involved and how we should never be alone together and also how we shouldn't use terms like *dating* or *boyfriend*. Being that it was the nineties, those terms hadn't been evangelically outlawed yet. I was, honestly, stoked out of my mind.

"I love it," I replied.

"Good . . . then you're going out with me this weekend," she said. John Hughes couldn't have written it better.

I went out with her. Being that it was the mid-1990s, I put on my most attractive pair of faded denim jeans, my most Soundgarden-esque work boots, and a splash of Drakkar Noir that I borrowed from a friend whose room smelled like whatever depressing New Jersey industrial site they use to manufacture Drakkar Noir, which is to say that my friend wore a lot of cologne all the time and so did his roommate.

Being that it was the midnineties, Kristin and I didn't

have cell phones and thereby weren't in constant textual communication leading up to the time that she was supposed to pick me up in the lobby of Wengatz Hall. She was almost a half hour late for the predetermined pickup time, which left me sitting forlornly in the lobby beneath the oil painting of whatever rich guy had funded the building. I figured she forgot, or didn't like me, or had met somebody else.

But when she walked in, it was all worthwhile. The other hot nineties girl thing was sundresses, and being that it was spring and the kind of warm Taylor day that made *Portlandia*-type guys take their shirts off and play Frisbee, she was wearing a tan sundress with little ladybugs printed all over it. She was backlit by the sunlight that streamed in the doors at Wengatz Hall. She smelled like someplace exotic.

Three months later we were engaged.

What happened in between was lots of sowing of the seeds of idolatry. In our limited theological economies, it was, like, *so obvious* that God meant for Kristin and me to come to Taylor so that we could find each other and get married. We spent three months worshipping each other. I watched *Say Anything* and then did my best to Lloyd Dobler her right to the altar. It worked.

Being that we had limited theological economies, we were convinced God would quote/unquote bless the fact that we had nobly—barely—managed to not have sex before our wedding.

I was twenty.

Being adored (while also adoring another) was a narcotic,

and I wanted it all the time. We uttered lots of phrases like "you're perfect!" to each other in lots of cinematic, Midwestern romantic moments.

I was out of my mind with longing for one person. The world was my oyster, and suddenly life was full of hope and possibility because I had a girl who was hot and who also adored me. Because of that, I could do anything I ever wanted and no matter what happened we would always be fine because we would always have each other.

Being that I was the young, arrogant, naive, and stupid Grunge Bosworth, I thought I could be everything to Kristin all the time, managing to fill our lives with enough money, enough cool trips, enough great sex, enough people-pleasing tranquility, and enough public acclaim to keep her perpetually happy.

For a while—a long time, actually—we were happy with this arrangement. We moved a lot. We lived in Eastern Europe for a while. We worked. I played semipro football and embarked on the romantic end of a writing career, in which I was submitting poetry the old-fashioned way, via letters that went through actual mail, and occasionally getting published. We dreamed of a book deal or multiple book deals. She believed in me and, being that we were in our twenties, life seemed full of possibility.

My idol, in a sense, was Kristin, . . . but it was also being *her idol*. And as idols always do, I fell off my pedestal. We both might have been better prepared for this if we had taken the story of Jacob and Rachel and Leah to heart.

JACOB AND THE IDOL OF ROMANCE

The lie that it is possible to have an apocalyptic romance[7] in which both parties solve all of each other's problems and manage, against all odds, to fulfill one another in every way imaginable is the lie embedded in every piece of pop/American/marriage/love entertainment. The story of Jacob and Rachel was perhaps the first documented case of the Apocalyptic Romance and the idolatry of your spouse. Genesis 29 reads:

> *While he was still talking with them, Rachel came with her father's sheep, for she was a shepherd. When Jacob saw Rachel daughter of his uncle Laban, and Laban's sheep, he went over and rolled the stone away from the mouth of the well and watered his uncle's sheep. Then Jacob kissed Rachel and began to weep aloud. He had told Rachel that he was a relative of her father and a son of Rebekah. So she ran and told her father.*
>
> *As soon as Laban heard the news about Jacob, his sister's son, he hurried to meet him. He embraced him and kissed him and brought him to his home, and there Jacob told him all these things. Then Laban said to him, "You are my own flesh and blood."*
>
> *After Jacob had stayed with him for a whole month, Laban said to him, "Just because you are a relative of mine, should you work for me for nothing? Tell me what your wages should be."*

Now Laban had two daughters; the name of the older was Leah, and the name of the younger was Rachel. Leah had weak eyes, but Rachel had a lovely figure and was beautiful. Jacob was in love with Rachel and said, "I'll work for you seven years in return for your younger daughter Rachel."[8]

There's no telling why Jacob agreed to work for an entire seven-year period. Perhaps Rachel was too young, or perhaps Jacob just wanted to demonstrate the depth of his commitment to her. At any rate, we're told that because of the depth of his idolatry/obsession, the time flew by.

Laban said, "It's better that I give her to you than to some other man. Stay here with me." So Jacob served seven years to get Rachel, but they seemed like only a few days to him because of his love for her.
Then Jacob said to Laban, "Give me my wife. My time is completed, and I want to make love to her."[9]

Jacob isn't shy here regarding his obsession and his intentions. Awkward?

So Laban brought together all the people of the place and gave a feast. But when evening came, he took his daughter Leah and brought her to Jacob, and Jacob made love to her. And Laban gave his servant Zilpah to his daughter as her attendant.[10]

We can only assume that Leah was wearing some kind of veil or that Jacob was so, um, *compromised* (read: hammered) after a night of feasting/partying that he wasn't aware of whom he was sleeping with. Either way, morning must have been a rude awakening.

When morning came, there was Leah! So Jacob said to Laban, "What is this you have done to me? I served you for Rachel, didn't I? Why have you deceived me?"

Laban replied, "It is not our custom here to give the younger daughter in marriage before the older one. Finish this daughter's bridal week; then we will give you the younger one also, in return for another seven years of work."

And Jacob did so. He finished the week with Leah, and then Laban gave him his daughter Rachel to be his wife. Laban gave his servant Bilhah to his daughter Rachel as her attendant. Jacob made love to Rachel also, and his love for Rachel was greater than his love for Leah. And he worked for Laban another seven years.[11]

Needless to say, it had to be tough to be Leah in this situation, but even today, under less weird/drastic circumstances, there are women who feel trapped in bad marriages, desperate to win the affection of the men in their lives.

When the LORD saw that Leah was not loved, he enabled her to conceive, but Rachel remained childless.

Leah became pregnant and gave birth to a son. She named him Reuben, for she said, "It is because the LORD has seen my misery. Surely my husband will love me now."[12]

This story illustrates that idolizing another is as common as the heart itself. We see it in Jacob's obsession with Rachel and in Leah's need to have Jacob's genuine love. We see something of ourselves in their story. Leah thinks that a child will solve her problems. Jacob thinks that if only he has Rachel, everything will be okay, and everything he went through will have been "worth it." Pop culture tells us that "I can't live without you" is the sexiest thing someone could possibly say. And that nothing could be better than hearing it. In human terms, this is true. It's a thrill. It can actually become an addiction. But it's a temporal thrill. And the Bible tells us that it's idolatry, and idolatry is sin.

The question is, how do we identify, unmask, and crucify this sin?

FALLING OFF THE PEDESTAL

Like many Americans, Kristin and I bought too much house too soon, a decision that would both haunt us as well as provide ample opportunity to be on our knees, praying and wondering how God would intervene when it looked like we couldn't pay our bills (and sometimes actually couldn't). The name of our subdivision is Village Place.[13] I don't even know what that means. I vowed I would *never* live in the suburbs, and we moved here seven years ago. And here's the thing—I love it. I love how quiet is. I love the banal chitchat I make with my neighbors. I love the lack of sirens at night. I love that I don't have four locks on my front door. I love that I can let my kids run across the street to play and know they'll be okay.

During this time we were also, silently, battling infertility. We tried for seven years, in vain, to get pregnant. Infertility impacted our relationship—and our idolatry of each other—because it was the first sign of imperfection. It was the first instance in which we had to reckon with the fact that God might exist for a purpose other than giving us everything we wanted and making all of our dreams come true. Simply put, it wrecked us.

Scene 1: I'm walking through the third-floor lobby of the Sparrow Medical Clinic in downtown Lansing, which houses the Sparrow Fertility Clinic. Married for several years now. I've been provided a standard-issue blank Styrofoam cup, much like the kind you would get at a mall food court or a gas station when you order a fountain pop. Except that inside this one is a small clear plastic jar into which I'm sup-posed to provide a sample, which is part of a yearlong fertility "journey" (this is what they call it in the brochures), which started after we adopted our first son, Tristan, and officially ended just before the adoption of our second son, Maxim, but in reality will never really end. On paper, that's a five-year period. Spiritually, it's much longer.

The unfortunate thing about the walk through the lobby

with the cup is that I run into a friend who is a doctor in the same building, and with whom I have to make awkward chitchat while at the same time holding the "sample" in the Styrofoam cup. My face gets red and I begin to sweat. It occurs to me that "producing a sample" used to be the thing about which teenage boys would giggle and lie to each other. Today is the feeling that it's just sort of sad, required, and hopeless. It's an assignment. It occurs to me that there's a lot of hopeless, pointless flailing in my life, trying to get to something I can't quite have.

Scene 2: Years' worth of slightly-to-moderately crazy fertility treatments haven't worked, and we're seated in the small office of the Midwest's foremost authority on fertility. In my hand I have a paper clip that I'm fidgeting with furiously. It's hotter than normal in the office, and the doctor—bald and in his midfifties—has a bead of sweat on his brow. His glasses are crooked. He looks crazy, but there are, like, fifteen degrees on the wall in his office and the requisite pictures of him with semifamous and important people, pictures that all middle-aged men have in their impressive offices. At some point he says, "I can get you pregnant," as though he were God and had control over such things.

We do boxer shorts, herbals, Clomid, a crazy operation, and artificial insemination. After several years and lots of money, he never gets us pregnant.

The infertility years bring with them several published books, a few awards,[14] and just enough success to keep me chasing after the next hit of The Praise of Man. Kristin says things like, "I'm glad to be doing this[15] for you . . . I believe in your writing career," but I don't believe her because of how sad she is about infertility and how worried we always are about money. She sometimes goes into her room, closes the door, and stays there for hours. It occurs to me that I'll never understand what it means, to a woman, to want to carry a child, just as she'll never understand why I want to get into a ring and fight or put on a helmet and keep playing football. Sometimes I'm mad at Kristin for not being content with the life that I've worked so hard to provide. Sometimes I'm so full of sympathy and sadness that I stay up half the night and pray for her.

She says things like, "I'll never be a real woman, because I haven't carried a child." She talks about the pain of playdates and baby showers and even just going to church. I try to understand. I try to tell her that her womanhood, and her success as a wife, isn't defined by something like carrying a child for nine months. She doesn't believe me.

She tells me that my manhood isn't defined by the kind of house we live in, or whether or not I'm "tough." I won't believe her. What I will believe is that I am no longer her idol. She no longer, operatively, has anyone to worship. And I no longer have a wife who will worship at the altar of me. We take on a life of satisfied dissatisfaction. We still love the same movies, the same foods. The same things make us laugh. But inwardly we're both nursing secret hurts and insecurities that we're afraid to verbalize, because to do so would be to indict the other as imperfect. I'm hurt and insecure because we couldn't get pregnant. She's hurt and insecure for the same reason. I'm hurt because I'm no longer her idol. We're both hurt because it looks like our romance wasn't "enough" to fulfill each other's hopes and dreams. So we mostly stay silent.

We both retreat inward, into our own pain and our own secret worlds where the economy of those worlds is defined by things that hurt us (infertility, professional failure) and things that make us feel good (boxing and football, for me) and things that make us feel good even though they hurt us (boxing, again, and private sins).

It occurs to me, during these dark weeks, that the losses we'd experienced—a failed adoption, failed book deals, failure to get pregnant—were more significant than I had once thought. I did not deal correctly with the losses. My coping method was more fun. More bottles of wine in the evening, more dinner parties, and more plans. I never developed a theology of suffering, meaning that I never bothered to wonder how and why God might use these losses and disappointments to drive me to closer dependence on Him. I never encouraged Kristin to deal with the deep issues, and our marriage suffered.

TAKING ROMANCE, AND OURSELVES, OFF THE THRONE

Romance is, well, *romantic*, for a reason. It feels awesome to be someone else's idol, and it's intoxicating to idolize another person. Everything in the media and in our culture confirms you in this flush of infatuation. For a time, you feed off each other's energy. This intoxication makes this idol one of the hardest household gods to flee.

We first need to make sure our worship of God isn't clouded by our worship of another person. For those of us who are romantics, it can be hard to think this way, and hard to read Paul writing so unromantically about marriage. Only God's love is perfect. When you're in the throes of love, it's hard to believe that the other person could or would ever disappoint you. But he or she will.

Second, I think we should take seriously Paul's assertion that not everyone should marry and what this implies about how we view marriage. Writing in 1 Corinthians 7:32-34 he said, "I would like you to be free from concern. An unmarried man is concerned about the Lord's affairs—how he can please the Lord. But a married man is concerned about the affairs of this world—how he can please his wife—and his interests are divided." Considering this passage may not only change how we think of and treat singles in our churches but also how we approach our own relationships, because it speaks to the idea that marriage isn't the be-all and end-all of Christian existence. This is an idea worth exploring—whether we are single or married.

Finally, we shouldn't be surprised by trials in our marriages and families. We sometimes think that if we meet and marry The One, our lives will take on a fairy-tale quality as we just move from one success to another. This isn't true. If it were, we'd be our own gods. God allows trials to test and strengthen our faith, to refine us, and to conform us to the image of Christ. This can't happen without hardships. The Bible is full of support for this idea, yet we still feel affronted when it happens.

Hebrews 12:7 reads, "Endure hardship as discipline; God is treating you as his children." But in verse 11, we see the fruit of the pain: "No discipline seems pleasant at the time, but painful. Later on, however, it produces a harvest of righteousness and peace for those who have been trained by it."

James told us that maturity and completeness of character is our goal, when he wrote, "Consider it pure joy, my brothers and sisters, whenever you face trials of many kinds, because you know that the testing of your faith produces perseverance. Let perseverance finish its work so that you may be mature and complete, not lacking anything."[16]

As hard as it sometimes is to believe, this is a higher goal than a beautiful or handsome spouse, perfect kids, and a scrapbook full of family memories.

⇒ From Kristin ⇒

I was shamelessly obsessed with boys from kindergarten on (and I don't specifically remember before kindergarten, although I can guess I was then too). I didn't even try to pretend that I was one of those smart, independent girls who didn't care if I got married or not—I wanted to get hitched. ASAP. I think I was about thirteen when I told my mom, with the dead earnestness of that age, that I thought I was ready for a serious relationship. I didn't have a ton of "dating success" in high school (meaning the guys I liked didn't like me, and I didn't like the invariably nerdy guys who all asked me to the Christian-school-prom-equivalent banquet five months early). I arrived at the Christian Marriage Mart bright-eyed and hopeful that I would meet The One at welcome weekend.

Fast-forward to Christmas break my senior year, when my brothers and their rosy-cheeked girlfriends and my parents all had to put up with my moodiness and epic tantrums, brought on by my sense of romantic failure and my terror about my looming future. I had no idea what I wanted to do. I had always vaguely seen myself as the snappily dressed mom who keeps her figure and makes the best cookies for the school bake sale! I was furious that I was going to have to figure it out and do it, whatever it was, all by myself.

I had had my share of dead-end relationships: tried being the nice-girl-you-bring-home-to-mom, and when that didn't work, I even made a halfhearted attempt at being the hot-devil-may-care-party-girl. That definitely fell flat, because I was neither hot nor devil-may-care, nor did I know how to party. I never quite fit in with either the popular kids or the nerdy kids. As a semirebellious idealist given to protracted esoteric thoughts, I lived in a sort of weird social netherworld that just didn't offer a lot of dating choices. But I always wanted to get married to a nice Christian guy who wasn't too nerdy, who would love me and take the pressure off of me having to have a career.

Marriage was something I felt I had to have, something I deserved, and if God didn't give it to me (especially in light of what a Good Girl I had been most of my life!), then what good was He anyway? I spent spring break interviewing for jobs I didn't want. A depressing glimpse of my future. I came back to college, ready to just get through and get on to the next horrible stage. Enter Ted. Tall, smart, athletic, wildly charismatic, with awesome nineties hair, cool grunge clothes, and a streak of angst balanced by a disarmingly sweet tribute to how much he loved his parents. I was utterly smitten. And wonder of wonders, he adored me too. We spent hours talking, gazing into each other's eyes, dreaming about our future. We were instant soul mates. We were going to change the world. We were going to beat the odds. I just knew we could do anything, with the Power of Our Love. I gushed, I swooned, I flirted madly, I sickened everyone near us with my sheep eyes, I terrified my family with my headlong rush to the altar, but *this* was *it*! I had finally found The One, and he was even better than I had dared to hope for. I told people, "He's not perfect, but he's perfect for me!" and I meant it, except that I did think he was perfect. One of Ted's greatest sources of perfection was how perfect he thought I was. I loved having him as my idol, and I loved being his. It was a beautiful gift from God, but it was no substitute for God Himself. And it was God's mercy to me, and to him, to tear him and our love off its pedestal.

CHAPTER 3

You Should Be So Proud

THE HOUSEHOLD GOD OF LIVING YOUR DREAMS THROUGH YOUR KIDS

And the things of earth will grow strangely dim,
in the light of His glory and grace.
— LYRICS FROM "TURN YOUR EYES UPON JESUS"

It's such a day of contrasts, a spiritual mash-up of good and evil. It's sixty-five degrees outside and sunny. Perfect. Our supernice quarterback, who has kind parents, freckles, and a bit of a speech impediment, is having the day of his life. His mother will come to me in tears after the game and thank me for coaching her son. Also perfect. I'll tell her that it's a joy coaching him and that he was an absolute soldier on the field. I'll mean every word of it. I'll imagine them buying him pizza and making much of him, as they should.

I'm reminded of the flip side when, while coordinating our defense, I am relayed a message on the field from the Grand Ledge Area Youth Football League (GLAYF) board, which holds court in the booth perched atop the stands, explaining that I am to wear my officially licensed GLAYF ball cap in a forward-facing manner.

"What?" I respond to my coaching colleague as I try to get one player to get in a good stance, find another player's disappearing mouthpiece, and get another to stop spinning in circles. And these clowns are concerned about my hat? In the same league where coaches routinely cuss kids out on the sidelines and encourage dirty play, even among fourth graders?

I throw my hat to the sidelines. I'm angry. They're having a meltdown about my *hat*?

There's also the issue that my Clay Matthews-esque long hair looks better and is more contained in a backwards-facing hat.

Vanity of vanities, all is vanity.

I also roll my eyes at the clowns in the press box, which I'll later rightfully feel guilty for. I will say things about them to my wife and the other coaches that I'll regret. Again, rightfully. There is something holy and right about the guilt and conviction that comes from the Holy Spirit.

I got fired up about someone telling me how to wear my hat. Why do I care so much about my appearance? Am I vain? Probably. Am I just being rebellious for the sake of being rebellious? Perhaps. The point is that I care *way* too much about myself, and I care *way* too much about my son's football experience. I'm not alone in this.

Football has been great for my son. It's taught him to work through discouragement, to take instruction from others, and to work as a part of a team. And we've had pure joy together with this game—running sprints together after practice and throwing "sideline" patterns to each other until it gets too dark to see the ball. I thank God for this.

I wonder if any of the sets of harried parents I see at the game are happy. Many of those sets of parents are moving in separate directions, with separate children doing separate organized sports. Most are frowning. There are dads who spend their entire day here, at the field, away from their families, watching other peewee games to which they have no tangible connection.

There's no team in our team, as every child is his own little franchise. After the game each boy will go to his set of parents, who will privately and personally evaluate their child's performance. There will be no cross-family congratulating. One family will be disappointed—in spite of our big win—because their son's touchdown run was wiped out by a penalty. He hangs his head in disappointment. Another mom won't speak to our head coach because her son, who clearly hates football, didn't play much.

It's Sunday and I missed church. Is it worth it? I seriously doubt that it is.

COVETOUSNESS AND IDOLATRY

Today I'm meditating on Ephesians 5, which equates covetousness with idolatry, the same idolatry that means "having other gods before me" and is forbidden in the Ten Commandments. We humans have a proclivity toward taking the things that we want (covet) and making gods out of them. Nowhere is the similarity between the things we want and the things we worship more clear to me than on the football field in Grand Ledge, and in my own heart.

On a seemingly idyllic fall day in a classic American setting, we parents idolized our children. We coveted victorious experiences for them—and for *us*. Victory for our kids means *we* succeeded as parents. We parents crave the pats on the back that come with our child scoring the winning touchdown. We crave the looks of knowing pride from other parents who are happy that we've won but are also wishing it had been their kid reveling in the victory.

I'm reminded of the old hymn "Turn Your Eyes Upon Jesus," and the line that says, "And the things of earth will grow strangely dim, in the light of His glory and grace." At one time football was the brightest thing in my life. Putting on a jersey, competing, and *identifying* with football seemed to be the biggest, brightest, and most important thing a person could do. But that afternoon at the field there was a strange dimness to all of it. I realized I really would rather be sitting in church than on a football field on a beautiful fall day.

THE LORD GIVES, THE LORD TAKES AWAY

While we tend to equate this household god of "living your dreams through your kids" with ball fields and performing arts stages, this idol starts in the heart. It starts when we think that we're *owed* kid-related joy. It starts when we forget that the Lord gives and takes away. This is something that Abraham and Sarah struggled with.

This ancient couple felt the unique sorrow and heartache that accompanies long-term infertility. Childbearing was at the heart of the female experience, just as leaving a legacy was at the heart of the male experience. This hasn't changed. Eavesdrop on nearly any group of married women in their twenties or thirties and talk inevitably turns to labor-and-delivery stories.

Genesis 15 lays the groundwork for Abraham's journey of faith:

> *After this, the word of the LORD came to Abram in a vision:*
>
> > *"Do not be afraid, Abram.*
> > *I am your shield,*
> > *your very great reward."*
>
> *But Abram said, "Sovereign LORD, what can you give me since I remain childless and the one who will inherit my estate is Eliezer of Damascus?" And Abram said, "You have given me no children; so a servant in my household will be my heir."*[1]

In this vision God first reaffirms His goodness. He affirms that He is to be loved and trusted and not feared. Abraham then lays out his practical concerns before the Lord. Abraham believed that God cares about our needs, great and small, and his trust is an inspiration.

*Then the word of the LORD came to him: "This man
will not be your heir, but a son who is your own flesh
and blood will be your heir." He took him outside and
said, "Look up at the sky and count the stars—if indeed
you can count them." Then he said to him, "So shall
your offspring be."*

*Abram believed the LORD, and he credited it to him
as righteousness.*[2]

In spite of Abraham's positive interactions with the Lord,
and in spite of the Lord's promises, the narrative takes a dark
turn, and we see the ruinous effects of Sarah's obsession with
motherhood.

I don't know what it was like to be childless in Abraham
and Sarah's culture. But I know what it's like in ours. For
the married Christian woman, motherhood is the ultimate
dream. "Do you have some *news* for me?" one woman asks
another in the church lobby. Recently married couples
often get asked, "When are you going to . . . start?" For
the Christian woman, motherhood is always in the air—we
can only assume it was the same for Sarah, and her obsession
is clear:

*Now Sarai, Abram's wife, had borne him no children.
But she had an Egyptian slave named Hagar; so she
said to Abram, "The LORD has kept me from having
children. Go, sleep with my slave; perhaps I can build a
family through her."*[3]

This is where, as the spiritual leader of his family, it would have been good for Abraham to disagree vehemently with his wife. But we know that Sarah was very beautiful and, in that way that wives are, probably very persuasive. Our idols—and our spouse's idols—are not easily knocked off their pedestal.

> *Abram agreed to what Sarai said. So after Abram had been living in Canaan ten years, Sarai his wife took her Egyptian slave Hagar and gave her to her husband to be his wife. He slept with Hagar, and she conceived.*
>
> *When she knew she was pregnant, she began to despise her mistress. Then Sarai said to Abram, "You are responsible for the wrong I am suffering. I put my slave in your arms, and now that she knows she is pregnant, she despises me. May the LORD judge between you and me."*[4]

Sarah's broken heart, cynicism, and rage is palpable here. Her idolatrous plan has backfired, and the existence of a child, rather than encouraging her, has enraged her. Genesis 17 shows us the shock Abraham and Sarah experienced when they were visited by the Lord and told of their impending pregnancy:

> *God also said to Abraham, "As for Sarai your wife, you are no longer to call her Sarai; her name will be Sarah. I will bless her and will surely give you a son*

by her. I will bless her so that she will be the mother of nations; kings of peoples will come from her."

Abraham fell facedown; he laughed and said to himself, "Will a son be born to a man a hundred years old? Will Sarah bear a child at the age of ninety?" And Abraham said to God, "If only Ishmael might live under your blessing!"[5]

When the Lord told the couple that they would conceive, they were incredulous, even understandably cynical. Perhaps they had been through the false hope and ups and downs of close calls. At some point during infertility, you just shut off that part of your heart. Laughter may have been Abraham and Sarah's way of protecting themselves from more disappointment.

Abraham figured Ishmael was his best shot.

Then God said, "Yes, but your wife Sarah will bear you a son, and you will call him Isaac. I will establish my covenant with him as an everlasting covenant for his descendants after him. And as for Ishmael, I have heard you: I will surely bless him; I will make him fruitful and will greatly increase his numbers. He will be the father of twelve rulers, and I will make him into a great nation. But my covenant I will establish with Isaac, whom Sarah will bear to you by this time next year." When he had finished speaking with Abraham, God went up from him.[6]

Then, when Abraham was given Isaac, he nearly worshipped the boy, understandably. Anyone who has a child can relate to this dynamic. I adore my boys. To me they are beautiful creations, even when they're testing my patience.

We all know how the narrative plays out. Abraham is asked to do the unthinkable—to sacrifice his dear, beloved son, for whom he hoped, dreamed, and prayed. And astonishingly, he is willing to do so. He goes up the hill and prepares a sacrifice. But then the Lord provides a ram and a way out.

Did Abraham idolize his son? It's hard to say, but the scriptural narrative indicates that he did. As a culture, do we, sometimes, place our children on a pedestal? Probably. Is it sometimes easier to just agree with my wife, like Abraham did with Sarah, than to stand up to her and risk upsetting the balance of peace in the household? Probably. Is this, in some way, family idolatry? Definitely.

As the narrative comes to a close, Abraham is rewarded for his obedience:

> *The angel of the* LORD *called to Abraham from heaven a second time and said, "I swear by myself, declares the* LORD, *that because you have done this and have not withheld your son, your only son, I will surely bless you and make your descendants as numerous as the stars in the sky and as the sand on the seashore. Your descendants will take possession of the cities of their enemies, and through your offspring all nations on earth will be blessed, because you have obeyed me."*[7]

BECOMING LESS

How can we, as a family, be more intentional about thanking God for the circumstances He's put us in, regardless of how many children we have or how our kids measure up to the other children in our churches, on our athletic fields, and in our small groups?

Athletic fields, performing arts auditoriums, and hospital delivery rooms are, of course, only a few places where family idolatry subtly emerges. The idolatry present in such contexts is subtle because these activities are almost universally celebrated, even within our evangelical subculture. The things we want most—the stuff of perfect families—are the things we can't live without (idolize).

So how do we fight this? Do we run and escape? Maybe.

Perhaps the answer—or at least the beginning of an answer—can be found in John 3:30, which reads, "He must become greater; I must become less." I am always tempted to pursue and then herald my own greatness. When I'm obsessed with my son winning a football game, or jealous of couples in my church who seem to be able to produce a child every year like clockwork, I am seeking to become greater. I want—through the victories of my children—to be seen as greater in the world's eyes. But it's when I become less—when I'm at an emotional or financial end—that Christ becomes great for me. When Abraham became less, by following God's call even when it meant giving up what he loved the most, God became great by providing a ram.

How are you seeking perfection, or seeking to become greater, through your children? How might God be calling you to become less?

 ⇌ *From Kristin* ⇌

I spent last year studying the life of Abraham via a wonderful study called Bible Study Fellowship. It's a great, structured, in-depth Bible study. Check it out!

As the idea of family idolatry was a new revelation to me, I saw the story of Abraham and Isaac in a new light. In light of this couple's natural desire to have a biological child and the extreme cultural emphasis placed on procreation in the ancient Middle East, it seems to me that God was setting Abraham and Sarah up for idolatry. Isaac was the tangible manifestation of all of God's promises to Abraham.

I can all too easily put myself in Abraham and Sarah's shoes. Actually, I don't really have to "put" myself there; I've lived it. We're not sure how old Abraham was when God first came to him and told him He would give him an heir, but assuming that he and Sarah probably got married when they were young, as was customary at the time, the cycle of hope and disappointment had been going on for a long time. They must have hoped and been burned by disappointment so many times that they had to harden themselves a bit just to deal with the disappointment, telling themselves they didn't want to get pregnant anyway. And then God comes along with His promise that they would have a son and raises those hopes again. So once again, they were back on the cycle of hope and disappointment, for another twenty-five years! That baby was the product of so many hopes, so many years of longing and dreaming, he was bound to be worshipped. Add to that the fact that all of God's promises of land, inheritance, future generations, the future Messiah—all those promises hinged on Isaac. It must have felt like loving Isaac, worshipping him, was a way of loving God and His promises. Yet in spite of this, God still required Abraham to crucify his idolatry, to recenter his worship on God Himself, not on the gift He gave. The only real surprise here is that God didn't have Abraham sacrifice Isaac multiple times.

When I am tempted to be frustrated with what feels like an impossible situation—this tension between loving a person and making that person an idol—it helps me to remember this is an ancient tension. It helps to know that people have struggled with this since biblical times, and that God has been their portion. There is no way to avoid this pitfall without a constant dependence on God's wisdom and help to love rightly.

I have to take these struggles, temptations, and idolatries to the Lord—almost daily in some seasons of life. Two of the Ten Commandments can be boiled down to: Don't love anything more than God. While I'm sure we're not the only Bible readers to have noticed the link between covetousness and idolatry, I feel some ownership in this truth since I've just discovered it in my own study of Scripture. Call it the thrill of discovery. But the thrill of discovery is dampened somewhat by my realization of how far I fall short of obeying these commandments.

Ancient Israel struggled with a more obvious idolatry than we do today—bowing down to statues and calling them gods. That would seem ridiculous to us, here and now, when our Age of Enlightenment minds can recognize that there is no inherent value or power in carved stone idols. Our sophisticated minds would never be that foolish. Instead, we crave—and worship—things that do "give us" something—money, prestige, comfort, pleasure, security, leisure, happiness, love, family. We look to these things as the ultimate good and as the things that will make us ultimately happy, which means that we're trusting in them. This means we're putting them in God's place. They have become idols. Of all the items in the above list of modern-day idols, family is the most confusing. It's a good thing, and a gift from God. From the very beginning, God designed families, by making marriage and by blessing/commanding them to be fruitful and multiply. The responsibility and privilege of family is one of the most precious in Scripture, yet does this make it exempt from the coveting/idolatry commands? No, but because family is something we should value and make a priority, it can be difficult to realize when we have crossed over the line into idolatry.

So, how can we recognize family idolatry? It's easiest

to recognize it in others, but it's critical that we see it in ourselves. An idolatrous attitude is not always clearly definable, primarily because it's incredibly personal. For the most part, it comes down to motives. For example, putting kids in sports can be idolatry for a family if the parents are trying to live their dreams through their kids, looking for significance in their kids' accomplishments, and prioritizing their time so that the children's pleasure and activities take precedence over all else. Another family's sports involvement may look exactly the same, but their motives may be to teach teamwork and sportsmanship or to get involved in their community as salt and light. For most of us, our desire to have our kids in sports is a mixture of some good motives combined with some bad. The tricky part of recognizing family idolatry is an honest self-evaluation, and killing the sin without renouncing your family and joining a convent.

It's this mixture of good and bad moments that keeps me coming back to the subtly idolatrous Bible study introductions/hen parties that are as much a part of being a woman in the church as baby showers, Mother's Day shout-outs from the pulpit, and casseroles at potlucks. If I left the Bible studies and the church, the idolatry would take over because I would no longer be exposed to the truth of the Word.

CHAPTER 4

Blue Chips

THE HOUSEHOLD GOD OF SPORTS AND FAMILY

As the black wave of Permian players moved out into the middle of the field, eight thousand other souls who had filled the home side rose to give a standing ovation. This moment, and not January first, was New Year's Day.

— FROM *FRIDAY NIGHT LIGHTS*

The American Ladder of Football Success drives many of us and creates idolatry in our hearts by promising a happiness and purpose that it can't deliver—both for parents and their athletic children alike. It's maybe a stretch to say that I was Johnny High School Football Star. I would stop way short of saying that people idolized me, but in small towns in the Midwest, successful varsity athletes are put on a pedestal of sorts. I got a letterman's jacket. My name was written in the paper and mentioned on the radio. I got letters from college recruiters. I felt the ego trip of having someone from the principal's office come and pull me out of class, and not because I was in trouble, rather because a real, live Adult wanted to try to persuade me to come to his college! I slid my considerable high school bulk out of the little desk and strutted past my classmates, all of whom were still trapped in General Business or Creative Writing or Algebra II. Trapped, as they were, with their paper bag–wrapped textbooks, spitballs, and acne. I was convinced that they were going to be trapped forever in Hartford City, Indiana, while my inevitable college football scholarship was going to take me someplace exotic and sexy like Muncie (Ball State) or Terre Haute (Indiana State) or if I was really lucky/blessed, Bloomington (Indiana University).

God, as He often does, had other plans. A broken leg sustained in practice kept me on crutches and off the field for the majority of the fall. The letters that daily appeared in my mailbox eventually slowed to a trickle. Somebody else won the Rotary Club Football Award, which, ridiculously, was devastating for me, meaning that I spent the car ride home from the ceremony, and the next day, being surly and truculent to my parents, and, because competition/winning was a family idol, they understood and even sort of affirmed me in my devastation.

I didn't even make All-Conference. The Big School scholarship that I thought was inevitable never came. My fallback plan was to go to a small Christian college and be the King of the Jungle for a season or two there, and then transfer someplace "real." Instead I went to a small Christian college, broke my leg again, had surgery, battled depression and massive social anxiety, and for the first time was confronted with the elusiveness of my two most precious idols: football and being awesome.

I idolized football because I loved, and still love, nearly everything about the game. As a kid I used to lay out my football jerseys on the floor, put a record on my Fisher-Price turntable, and sit in my rocking chair, dreaming of wearing the jersey and what I would do in it. I love the aesthetics of the game. The helmets—Riddells, Schutt Airs, Adams Pro Elites, and even obscure brands like Rawlings and Maxpro. I love the jerseys—MacGregor Sand-Knit, Champion Mesh, and Nike Pro Combat. I love the exhausted feeling after practices and games. This affects my family because try as I may to explain or quantify my love of the game, Kristin can't understand it and, understandably, feels threatened by it. She feels threatened by the time and energy I expend loving it. She feels threatened by the depth of my disappointment when I lose. She feels threatened by how much I need it. And, finally, she feels threatened because she sees the same love of the game in our son Tristan.

DOES GOD OWE ME?

I idolized being awesome because who doesn't love being awesome? I was never *really* awesome. I was never a national football phenomenon, not even close. But after football I missed being *sought after*. I missed old guys at church asking me about the game, or how I was feeling. I missed having something to dream about while I listened to music.

I was only a college freshman, but I was no longer a football player. I was what I used to derisively call a "regular kid."

I idolized football, but I would have told you I didn't. I thought idolatry was worshipping a little gold calf or something, and I knew I didn't do that. I didn't drink, get high, or chase girls either. I figured God owed me. I figured He owed me the successful football career and "platform" that came with it—so that I could do meaningful evangelistic work like Sharpie-ing a cross on my wrist tape and kneeling in the end zone after touchdowns. I had no idea how to "make God my all," even though I was familiar with the language and had even learned to speak it quite well.

Instead, God gave me my first of a life's worth of lessons in Killing Your Idols 101 by allowing the broken leg that would sideline me for the rest of my college career. I desperately needed this to happen, even if I didn't yet realize it. I learned (eventually) that God would sustain me without football. I learned (eventually) that He could even use me in other ways. Today I'm incredibly grateful for this lesson, even if, at the time, I hated it.

Even so, my love of sports and competition affects my family.

PARENTING AND THE LOVE OF WINNING

The Playmakers track program is, perhaps, the most culturally diverse three hours in the Greater Lansing Area. Drawing inner-city and suburban track clubs from all over mid-Michigan, the program is everything from a way to get kids out of the house and active in the summer to an incubator for Olympic hopefuls, as some of the program's runners have made the Olympic trials.

Our youngest son, Maxim, is six years old but looks like he's four. He weighs all of thirty-three pounds soaking wet and is so skinny that his little blond head looks like an orange sitting atop a toothpick. He gets blown over in a stiff breeze. Our goal, for Maxim, is that he runs his races—tonight the 70 and the 100—without getting scared of the starter's pistol or stopping halfway to wave at us. He looks like a little elf and is a favorite of all of the younger-level coaches, most of whom are college girls. "Oh, Maxim!" they say, giggling, when he comes up to give them a hug. Lady-killer.

Our oldest son, Tristan, is nine and thinks he's twenty-two. Dressed in black shorts and a yellow Under Armour T-shirt, he's all business. Track spikes. Huge, brown, almond-shaped eyes focused on the task at hand, in today's case the 100- and the 70-meter dash. He competed in the long jump last year, and jumped eleven feet, seven inches, which was good enough to win several of these meets and bring him home a few miniature gold medals. Unfortunately, his success also put a target on his back and made him the object of derision for some of the inner-city track clubs. Simply put, these kids talk a lot of junk.

"You look fat in that tight shirt," says one. "You ain't worth (expletive), you can't run for (expletive)." This, of course, hurts his father much more than it hurts Tristan, and he won't tell me about it until we get into the car for the ride home.

As a football player I was punched, kicked, eye-gouged, and told things on the field that wouldn't be fit to print in any publication. I had much of my skin scraped off on bad Astroturf in dumpy little arenas all over the Midwest. I iced aching shoulders on horrendously long bus rides. I routinely called Kristin and said things like, "Never let me do this again," and, "If this is elite sports, I don't want Tristan to have any part of it."

But for the most part I love the sport and miss the competition desperately. I ache for it. It's what I dream about when I'm alone, listening to music, in the car. I don't dream of lake houses and new cars; I dream of cleats and receiver's gloves. Helmets. Teammates. Hearing the throbbing hip-hop music at the track and seeing my own sons warm up for their races takes me right back to the battle.

In truth, I'm praying that I can handle this—"this" being watching my sons competing in sports. The simple and wildly unspiritual truth is that I want my son to win. I want him to prove that he can hang with these kids, many of whom are running in Olympic-style unitards, and many of whose fathers are standing trackside, sporting Olympic-style scowls and wearing stopwatches around their necks.

Lord, help us to honor You with our effort and our behavior tonight, I pray with the boys, while we stretch. *And help me to control myself.* I pray the last part to myself and don't say it out loud. Tristan nods with my "amen." Maxim says, "Dad, can I have a Popsicle?" A steely-eyed competitor he isn't.

One of the dads from the other track clubs is putting his

kid through an elaborate series of stretches, pre-race. The kid is one of those wearing an Olympic-style unitard, gray with the word *Nike* emblazoned on the back. He's wearing a pair of Nike warm-up pants and Nike canary-yellow track spikes. He and his ex-athlete-looking (huge trapezius muscles, swagger) father are both frowning. This, to them, is war.

According to studies, of the thirty million or so children taking part in youth sports in the United States, only about two hundred will go on to be professionals in any given year.[1] But don't tell that to the fathers, and some of the mothers, of those kids. In this moment, we all believe our children have what it takes to be a part of that two hundred. What's more, we all desperately want our kids to be that good. Having tasted a little bit of pro sports, intellectually I *don't* want Tristan in that environment where feelings of depression, paranoia, and "Is this all there is?" rule the day. Feeling it in my heart is another thing entirely.

I'm standing at the end of the track, away from all the other fathers, struggling. I want Tris to feel God's joy when he competes, and when he runs "to feel His pleasure." I remember as a college athlete struggling through injuries, what a joy I felt at just being able to run again. But I can feel the war-nerve rising up in me. I want Tris to win and to crush his opponents. I want him to put people in their places. Then I remember he's nine, and I feel, for a moment, like the most ridiculous person in the world.

As he stands in his lane, I can see the other kids jawing at him. He's not jawing back. At that point I don't know that he's being trash-talked and cussed out. I'll find that out later. I notice that he's the only one not wearing tights on his legs. He's racing in an older age division this year, so I have the faint, pit-of-my-stomach feeling that this could be a rough season.

He settles into his stance, his calf muscles tensed. At the explosion of the pistol I hear nothing but the sound of my own heavy breathing. I'm not even running. For a minute, nobody in the world exists but my son and me. He really is a beautiful runner. He flies down the track, form perfect, face a mask of concentration and effort. I'm so proud I could explode. I thank God for sports, for track, for sunshine, and for the chance to compete. And then Tristan crosses the finish line. Sixth place.

He's crestfallen and, truth be told, I'm angry. I wanted to right the cosmic wrong of Little League psycho fathers by having my kid win. In the meantime, I had become the kind of Little League psycho father I detested.

We walk to the car in defeated silence. Maxim slurps on a Popsicle. He had been offered two Popsicles because he's so cute, but I declined the second one for him. He leapt into my arms as he crossed the finish line of his race, running alongside a high school girl who volunteered to make sure he made it all the way down the track and then gushed about how sweet he is. He came in last. Neither of us care.

"Dad, I've gotta tell you something," Tristan says quietly from the backseat. "These kids were saying some things to me tonight." And then he proceeds to fill me in on the trash talk. I'm so angry I'm close to going back to the field and ripping one of the smug father's faces off. I say some things I regret and have to apologize to Tris for later.

We've gotta get out of here.

"Here" being the suburbs, where sports idolatry is in full bloom and where I'm afraid I can't resist it. In one week I watched my friend's son play travel league baseball in uniforms as nice as those worn by the Detroit Tigers, had the aforementioned track meet, and interviewed for a peewee football coaching position in a process that was so rigorous (a nine-page application, How Do *You* See Yourself Enhancing the Grand Ledge Youth Football Tradition?) that you would think I was interviewing for a position with the Green Bay Packers.

Idolatry is alive and well in athletics, where making gods out of men sells tickets, pay-per-view packages, and over-priced track spikes to the fathers of six-year-olds. I've seen, as an athlete and a sports journalist, the absolute moral ruin that results when men and women, who were created *to* worship, end up *being* worshipped.

Given that I have long worshipped at the altar of winning in sports, it is no wonder that I struggle with making my children's success in sports an idol. I need an accountability partner. "Cory, this is Ted. I bought my six-year-old a pair of graphite track spikes that were made out of the same material they use on the space shuttle. They weigh half of an ounce and cost five hundred dollars. I think I need you to pray for me."

THE ALTAR OF SPORTS

I wanted Tristan to win in order to right the wrongs that I perceived had been done to him. I was using him as a weapon against the other athletes who talked too much and as my avenue to feeling good about myself through his winning. This is too much to put on a grade-schooler's shoulders, and it illustrates a parental heart that's in the wrong place.

I idolize sports whenever I idolize an athlete and expect his or her success. Am I disproportionately disappointed when my favorite athlete or team loses? Does it ruin my day or weekend and do I take that out on my family? If so, I may be worshipping at the altar of sport. Am I drawing more hope from Tim Tebow's celebrity and "platform" and athletic prowess than I am from the gospel? If so, I may be worshipping at the altar of sport.

Are sports compromising my ability to worship? If so, I am definitely worshipping at the altar of sport. (Keep in mind that the well-to-do older family in your church who disappears for four months every summer because they have a cottage up north may not be all that different from the young family who misses church every week because of youth football, travel baseball, or season tickets to the Lions.)

As a coach I've had film sessions and games on Sunday. And even on those Sundays when I went to church *before* the game, I confess I wasn't worshipping. I was wondering what to call on third-and-long. I know how difficult this issue is—and it's difficult because of how much I *love* football.

I idolize sports when I insist on having a "life of the body." When I say or think I can't be happy without some form of competition in my life. Competition, in and of itself, isn't the problem. The problem is when I *need* it in order to feel happy or peaceful.

PERFORMING ARTS AND FAMILY IDOLATRY

Ironically, on the same evening that I was dealing with child idolatry in the form of an irate sports father, I got to see the performing arts version of family idolatry firsthand.

When our local homeschool performing arts group wants to have a performance, they rent auditorium space from a huge public high school in order to accommodate all the parents and siblings in attendance, as these families aren't small and they tend to stick together.

I was seated in the third row of a mostly packed auditorium, observing the same dynamics (nervous parents, overly proud parents, and so on) that I observe and sometimes, sadly, perpetrate as a youth football coach.

The morose artist/poet in me loves these big, Made-for-Parents occasions. I like remembering my own big, childhood Made-for-Parents occasions and am excited for the participants. I envision their preshow nerves backstage and remember how that felt. I often end up staring sadly off into the distance and saying overly dramatic things to my wife—things like, "They'll never feel like this again; they will never again be in a packed room with a bunch of people cheering for them."

Kristin rolls her eyes and dutifully listens to me trying to articulate what it *is* about these events that bothers me so much: the programs listing the kids' names, the sad plate of store-bought cookies, the overly sweet punch, the congratulations. After all this hoopla the kids go back to being kids and stop being celebrities. And then they matriculate on to an adult life that comes and goes, largely without so much as a "good job" or a pat on the back.

In Angelo Pizzo's beautiful basketball film *Hoosiers*, the uptight Myrna Fleener, played by Barbara Hershey, confronts the new-in-town Norman Dale, a controversial basketball coach played by Gene Hackman, about the town's propensity toward idolizing basketball players. "A basketball hero around here is treated like a god," she says disgustedly. To which the coach replies, "Most people would kill . . . to be treated like a god, just for a few moments." God, it seems, is in the business of making sure we don't get to *be* our own gods.

"DEAR CHILDREN, KEEP YOURSELVES FROM IDOLS"[2]

Like me, God may be calling you to have no other gods before Him by taking a drastic step away from sports. As silly as this is to type, quitting my fantasy football league several years ago allowed me to reclaim many of my Sabbaths during football season. God may be asking me to take it a step further by stepping away from coaching, or at least modifying how and when I'm able to coach.

Though I fail so often, I want to be able to model to

my children a heart that longs after God. Too often, I fear, they see my heart longing after sports. The fallout is a heart divided—and a man who fails to love the Lord with all his heart, soul, and mind. My kids sometimes see me not being able to live without my sport, and not being able to live without winning. This is the wrong thing to model for them. How can I raise boys who long after the Lord, when they see me longing after something else?

Is it possible to love football without making it an idol? I'm on the verge of finding out. Can I thank God for the good gift of being able to play and coach without turning the good gift into a bad god?

I hope so. I pray so. Today my sons and I are at "The Schoolyard," which is an open field behind their school that has a tall, steep hill on the back of the property. We've just watched a documentary on former Chicago Bears running back Walter Payton (see: idols, childhood) who used to run hills in the off-season to train. I've laced on my all-white Pony seven-stud cleats (see: Namath, Joe) and we've jogged to the base of the hill on a day that is Michigan-perfect, seventy degrees and sunny, with a little breeze. Soon our shirts are off and we're all blasting up the side of the hill, trying to emulate my dead hero Walter Payton. This is football at its best. It's better than playing football in a stadium. It's better than getting letters from college football recruiters. It's way better, because it's me, my boys, and a heaping dose of pure joy from the Lord.

I want Tris to be ten forever, and Maxim to be seven forever, and for it to always feel exactly like this.

⇌ *From Kristin* ⇌

My relationship with sports has been sketchy, at best. My dad (who passed away a few years ago) was a sports nut, lettering in three sports in college—baseball, basketball, and football (where he was the captain). He went to a small college, but still—that's a lot of sports and my dad had a decent amount of talent. All his adult life he was an avid runner, completing a marathon the year he turned forty.

My dad was a sports fan, too, committed to his favorite teams. In fact, when I was growing up he was so obsessed with watching Michigan football on Saturday afternoons that I often joked that I could have walked through the living room naked and he wouldn't have noticed. And though I was joking, I believed it.

So it's strange that sports played such a minor role in my family when my two brothers and I were growing up. My brothers played some, here and there, but sports never ruled our schedule like it did so many other families'. I think this was my mom's doing. She was happy to date a stud athlete in college, but she didn't want her home filled with sweaty jockstraps and the dinner hour disrupted by tiresome sports practices.

I was never offered sports opportunities as a child (I was, after all, a girl—back then, in the South, it wasn't considered proper or worthwhile for girls to play sports), nor did I seek them out. I was content reading, baking, and acting out scenes from The Chronicles of Narnia with my girlfriends.

I don't like physical activity, and without the competitive element to push me, I would rather curl up with a book than jump around aimlessly. (Ted has told me that my capacity for sitting and reading is astonishing. Thank you very much.) So when I met Ted, I was a little conflicted. Let's be honest, athletes are hot. But then there is the dumb-jock factor, and that didn't appeal much to me. But then again, Ted was a "former" football player. And by former, I mean that he had been injured playing football and claimed he would never play again. I figured his being a former football player was a good thing, and since he would never play again—totally hated all sports, he assured me—I figured I could have all of the benefits of a cute athletic guy with none of the tiresome sports obsession.

A few months into our marriage Ted told me he was planning to drive across the country to try out for a professional football team, and I realized I had been duped. Not a former football player at all.

Since then our marriage has been a series of delicate negotiations that have included me spectating several seasons of semipro and professional football, allowing a boxing ring to be built in my basement, watching my husband vainly strive against his instinctive "Little League Dad" tendencies, freaking out when I look at the youth sports schedule, and realizing that watching sports can be fun if our priorities are in the right place.

As a parent, I not only try to encourage and help my

sons do their best in sports, but I'm also trying to keep watch over Tristan's and Maxim's souls. I try to walk that fine line between maintaining a positive perspective toward my boys' activities and sucking joy by doing the naggy, passive-aggressive mom thing where I "support" my kids while at the same time being sure to let them know I'm not enjoying it.

CHAPTER 5

On Writing and Grinding Concrete

THE HOUSEHOLD GOD OF VOCATION

I am not my own, but belong, body and soul, to my
faithful Savior, Jesus Christ.
— FROM QUESTION 1, HEIDELBERG CATECHISM

Hello, my name is Ted Kluck. I have written a dozen books,
am an adjunct professor at a local college, and recently earned
my masters of fine arts degree from an accredited institution
of higher learning. I just finished a ten-hour shift operating
a concrete grinder on a construction site, which, ironically,
is the Fine Arts building at a local college where I got to see
a group of full-time professors walking to class and living
the life I want to live (shoulder bag, hipster glasses) while I
was covered in sweat and concrete dust, living the life that
the Matt Damon character lived at the beginning of the film
Good Will Hunting.

   You might think I'm going to write about how noble and

good it is to work with my hands and eke out a humble living with my muscles and the sweat of my brow while I pursue full-time employment as a professor of creative writing. But I'm not going to do that, because I hate grinding concrete. I would trade it in a heartbeat for the opportunity to stand in front of a closet full of jeans, deciding which faux cowboy shirt to wear with which jeans as I get ready to stand before a room full of students who want to learn about writing. Make no mistake, I would like that better than grinding concrete.

Did I mention that in 2008 I won a Michigan Notable Book Award? I have no idea if this is a big deal, but I do know that I spent five of the last ten hours operating an upright concrete grinder, and the other five on my knees operating a hand grinder. The knee part was the worst, what with all the kneeling, getting up, and breathing dust despite my best efforts not to breathe the dust.

I had to haul the heavy machinery up and down a flight of stairs because the service elevator only went to 4 and I was working on 5. Bummer.

At one point one of the history professors (you'll know them by their Dockers and uncool shirts) wandered up to the floor I was grinding in order to "just let us know" that "some of the professors were complaining" about the noise my colleagues and I were generating with our concrete grinders. I nodded and listened intently, though he had no idea how much I related to what he was saying or knew how difficult it must have been for him to volunteer to walk up the flight of stairs to the attic part of the building to engage the dirt-covered guys in hard hats about how loud they were being. "They might shut you down," he said, gravely but courageously, like the kind of courage a kid uses when he takes off the training wheels for the first time. I smiled and tipped my hard hat at him in a gesture that was full of both understanding and a little derision, though I'm not sure he got the derision part, glad as he was to just be getting out of there.

Did I mention that I am still an adjunct? I'll be teaching four classes tomorrow. "How do you do that?" some of my teaching colleagues ask, referring to how I manage to teach freshman writing or freshman speech for that many hours in a row on Tuesdays and Thursdays and sometimes Friday morning (and sometimes online). What they don't know is how much I absolutely love it, and how grateful I am to be teaching, as compared to grinding concrete.

After the history professor left, all of us guys on the crew submitted our opinions on the noise in writing, then we had a committee meeting about the issue that was spirited but collegial and resulted in lots of shared meaning. Actually, none of that happened. What happened is that we just kept grinding because at the end of the day, the college was never going to shut us down, was it?

Did I mention that this chapter isn't really about writing or grinding concrete? It's about how badly I want a teaching job. I do. Really. Is teaching an idol for me? Maybe. It's something I've worked hard for and feel like I deserve. Sometimes I feel like I can't live without being able to teach. Sometimes

I wonder why my generation has such a hard time just going to work, obsessed as we are, with professional "fulfillment." And by "my generation" I kind of mean my generation, but I mostly mean me.

STEVE JOBS AND THE IDOL OF PROFESSIONAL SUCCESS

Jobs is a biopic about the life of Steve Jobs, former Apple computers scion and famous American entrepreneur. Jobs has become an American business hero/rock star, even though, in addition to his unquestioned intellect, creativity, and vision, he could also be arrogant, insensitive, and extremely selfish. I watched the film because I fancy myself a creative entrepreneur, even though few of my projects have made me much money, and even though the boutique publishing company I started a few years ago[1] has put out some truly great books, it has only made . . . wait for it . . . 3.5 *thousand* dollars. Steve Jobs, I'm not. What I feel like, most of the time, is a massive professional failure.

The film is of interest to me in part because everyone in the Jobs constellation—including Steve Wozniak and even Jobs himself—was burned and hardened by the experience of working with him. The film paints Jobs, rightly, as something of an ahead-of-his-time, tormented, artistic visionary, but also shows him to be vicious and ruthless in his pursuit of the Apple vision. Jobs was, in a nutshell, the archetypal American hero—bold, independent, and without a conscience most of the time. I was especially intrigued by the way he eventually parted ways with all of the friends who helped him start Apple. At one point in the film Wozniak, who created the first Apple computer, confronted his egotistical CEO, saying, essentially, "I can't even remember the last time you said 'hello' to me around here. All I wanted was to do something cool . . . and do it with my friends."

After watching the film I told Kristin, "I'm the Wozniak character." She immediately understood. All I've ever wanted out of writing is to write good books and do it with my friends, but the longer I live, the more I realize that's probably a pipe dream. As a result of the Fall, work is frustrating and heartbreaking. If it wasn't, we would be one step closer to being our own gods.

The Jobs dynamic—the subtle shafting of friends and the big-timing of people in pursuit of fame or success—is one that I've been on both sides of, in, believe it or not, Christian publishing, where people can be every bit as careerist and shallow and conniving as the people in corporate America. It's strange. Those of us who are entrepreneurs want to essentially *be* Steve Jobs, but those of us who are Christians should also find great sobriety and caution in his tale. His products have created a subculture, and his design elements have, for the time being, endured. But at what cost? Lost friends? Lost relationships?

According to the film, Jobs lost all of those. Especially chilling was the way he treated the mother of his daughter—seeing her presence as an intrusion and working as hard as he could to write her out of the story of his life.

He didn't have time for a wife and a child, and while the portrayal was somewhat over the top, in true Hollywood fashion, I can see these shortcomings in my own life. I can see the way I put my kids off in order to check one more e-mail. I can see how I take it out on them when things aren't going well at work.

Serving the idol of occupation takes its toll on our families.

VOCATION AS FULFILLMENT

It's not uncommon for men, especially suburban, affluent American men, to look to our jobs to fulfill us. We're taught to "chase our dreams" and "plan for the future" and create "our best life now."[2] Even the language of our so-called Christian superstars (such as Joel Osteen) muddies these waters. The promise is that if we're serving God, He is somehow required to set us up in a fulfilling career that supplies us with all that we need, materially. Consequently, we feel personally affronted when this doesn't work out.

Maybe you don't love your job. Maybe you do not make quite enough. Maybe you wonder why God has put you in this particular workplace or circumstance. Incidentally, I have wondered each of these things at one time or another. But what if it's God's mercy that things are not working out the way we had hoped? Perhaps He puts us in these situations to keep us humbly relying on Him.

What if we thought of our vocations as—instead of the conveyer of happiness and fulfillment—the thing that causes us to glory in our Redeemer? Think about it: If I'm so successful in my career that I go home each evening convinced of my own greatness (sounds nice, actually), this leaves no room for God to be glorified. Instead, if I'm challenged on a regular basis and am faithfully trusting in Him to clothe me, feed me, and meet my needs, then He gets glory, and I grow in closeness to my Lord.

BATTLING FOR PERSPECTIVE

There's an interesting parable at the beginning of Matthew 22 about a king who prepares a wedding banquet. Ostensibly, this guy spares no expense and kills the proverbial fatted calf. He wants so badly for people to come that he sends his servants out to round them up. This is, of course, a picture of believers and disciples going out to share the Good News in a hardened, selfish, and jaded world, and having it mostly fall on deaf ears. But it's the *reasons* people give for not going to the banquet that I find most chilling. Matthew 22:2-5 reads:

> *The kingdom of heaven is like a king who prepared a wedding banquet for his son. He sent his servants to those who had been invited to the banquet to tell them to come, but they refused to come.*
>
> *Then he sent some more servants and said, "Tell those who have been invited that I have prepared my dinner: My oxen and fattened cattle have been butchered, and everything is ready. Come to the wedding banquet."*

But they paid no attention and went off—one to his field, another to his business.

Luke's account in chapter 14, verses 18-20, goes into even greater detail on the invitees' excuse-making:

But they all alike began to make excuses. The first said, "I have just bought a field, and I must go and see it. Please excuse me."
Another said, "I have just bought five yoke of oxen, and I'm on my way to try them out. Please excuse me."
Still another said, "I just got married, so I can't come."

Jesus doesn't say that these people didn't come to the feast because they were busy engaging in drunkenness and orgies. That would be too easy, in a way, for us. We can look down on those things and say, "I don't do that, so I'm good." However, the reason these people had no time for the king and paid no attention to him is because they were busy *working* and *getting married*. That's convicting. They were attending to their obligations. In other (proper) contexts, the things they were doing were good.

When I read this parable, it causes me to ask, Am I missing the banquet because of my occupational obsessions? Am I missing valuable and precious years with my wife and children because I'm busy worrying about my job, wondering why I'm not more appreciated at work and obsessed with the fact that other people are? Am I missing the "forest" of what God is doing in me and for me because I can't see past the "trees" of what's bothering me at work?

BATTLING FOR JOY

Writing is not the Dream Job I thought it would be. I'm an introvert, meaning that I prefer to not work with people. I thought that writing from home would allow me to avoid people. I couldn't have been more wrong. Writing is maddeningly collaborative and endlessly frustrating. It seems that there's no end to the number of people you have to please and whom you may not even like.

What's more, I know that the teaching gig I so desired while grinding concrete (and *still* desire) won't be fulfilling either. It will, in fact, come with its own measure of frustration.

What if I consistently took my vocational frustration to the Lord in prayer? What if I asked Him to redeem the time I was spending and the products I'm trying (mostly in vain, it seems) to create? What if I asked Him to help me leave my work at the door when I entered the house so that I could focus on my wife and kids?

I'm setting a false and confusing example for my children if I proclaim to love the Lord with all my heart, and then they see me constantly worried about or obsessed with my work. I fear that I'm trusting God with my words, but not my actions.

What if I, boldly and like the psalmists, asked the Lord

for joy even in the midst of rough or unsatisfying circumstances? This, I believe, would keep God at the center and on the throne, rather than putting me—my talents, my desires, my sense of entitlement—at the center of my professional life. When I'm acting and worshipping in this way, I find it easier to be genuinely happy for those who do well in my field. I can be glad for my friends when they get book deals instead of acting as if I'm glad for them and then secretly resenting it.

The Heidelberg Catechism reminds me that I'm not my own. It reminds me to whom I belong, body and soul (and vocation). In this, even in professional heartache, I can have hope. I know that He "has set me free from the tyranny of the devil," and, I can infer, from the tyranny of whatever I'm facing in my work life. Finally, most comfortingly, "He also watches over me in such a way that not a hair can fall from my head without the will of my Father in heaven."[3]

In this I can work—teaching, writing, *or* grinding concrete. And in this I can rest.

↽ *From Kristin* ⇀

This Sunday our pastor was talking about how the disciples had ambition for the wrong thing—power in an earthly kingdom. And then he went on to apply that to misplaced ambitions in our lives, ambitions for wealth, power, fame. He went on to clarify that these things are not inherently wrong in and of themselves, and some devoted Christians do indeed gain those things, but that it is the lust for them, the chasing after them, the have-to-have-them, that is the problem. True, powerful, and convicting words.

It struck me that those examples—wealth, power, fame—are primarily male idolatries. Sure, women may want some of those things too, but when men sit around and fantasize, they are thinking about being the richest guy, the prodigy in their field, wielding power and influencing people, being known and respected. There may be a family, supporting and adoring, off to the side, but the substance of most men's fantasies is the accolades, the respect, the riches themselves. But for me, the sense of "this is my whole life, this is what I live for, this is what I dream of, this is what completes me and gives me significance" comes from having a family.

The church has long battled against men who are workaholics—or has at least appeared to be battling against men who are workaholics. This is considered a sinful lack of proper priorities, not because men should work less and be lazy but because there should be some dimension to what they do. Dads spend many hours a week working, where they cultivate talents, individuality, friendships, and people skills in an environment where their families are a footnote to who they are. Then they come home, and, if they're living right, engage with their families, cultivating a different side of themselves, leading to balance and well-roundedness.

Stay-at-home moms, of which I am one, work all

day with the kids and then . . . work all evening with the kids. Stay-at-home moms become deeply and completely immersed in parenting when it's the only thing they do. They sometimes struggle to cultivate themselves as individuals with any interests or work outside of raising the kids, and often their only friendships revolve around parenting as well (if moms do manage to be together without their kids, all they talk about is their kids). The topic of children, for many moms, is like sports for guys—it can be a "safe," semimeaningless topic of female conversation.

I was at a church meeting recently where we were asked to tell a few things we like to do, and all the women (all, incidentally, homeschooling moms) said they didn't have any hobbies or interests since they'd had children. While this could have been an example of spiritual one-upsmanship/martyrdom where people assume it's worldly to enjoy anything or make time for themselves, it seemed to me that these moms were just making sincere statements of the truth. One even said, "I used to have hobbies before I had kids, but now I don't have time for anything else."

Not only does this single focus lead to one-dimensional and possibly unhappy moms, it lends itself to idolatry. If people devoted the same amount of focus and time to their jobs as a moms do to their children, they would instantly be suspected of idolizing their jobs and of being workaholics. Put that much time and energy and effort into one thing, and it's sure to become an unhealthy obsession, whether you mean for it to or not. Being a stay-at-home mom is a vocation tailor-made for rampant idolatry. At least, that has been the case for me.

CHAPTER 6

Be Perfect

THE HOUSEHOLD GOD OF WINNING AT EVERYTHING

You shall not make for yourself an image in the form
of anything in heaven above or on the earth beneath
or in the waters below. You shall not bow down to
them or worship them; for I, the LORD your God, am
a jealous God.

— EXODUS 20:4-5

I identify with what Don DeLillo writes about losing in his
heralded novel *Underworld*:

> *He could not take the losing. It was too awful. It
> made him physically weak and massively angry. It sent
> him reeling through the flat, arms windmilling. His
> brother bopped him on the head and that made him
> madder. He did not have enough height and weight to
> contain all his rage. He was past the point of crying.*

*Losing made his limbs shake. He gasped for air. He
did not understand why someone so small, young, and
unprepared should have to squat in the path of this
juggernaut called losing.*[1]

"I can relate to that," I tell Kristin. "I've felt that way
nearly every time I've ever lost."

In the American sports culture, one of the first commandments we learn is to hate losing. Losing, we learn, should make us sick. Losing, we learn, is not acceptable. I bought into this particular commandment wholeheartedly.

Case in point:

I'm coaching fourth and fifth grade youth football again. Tonight, day three of practice in pads, we're scrimmaging another Grand Ledge team and are taking it on the proverbial chin. My son Tristan is a natural. A hitter. He unloads on the other players with perfect physics and creates the kind of pad-popping hits that make people on the sidelines go "ooh." Sadly, however, only a few other kids on the team enjoy contact, and we're getting shellacked in the scrimmage by a team coached by my friend Tim, who for the evening is not my friend but the guy who is sending blitzing linebackers in droves and making it impossible for me to run even the simplest of plays. I'm fuming. I played college football and arena ball and semipro ball, and Tim didn't. I should be winning and he should be losing.

My team slinks off the field, dejected. I say something uninspiring about "getting them next time." One of my players, a kid with glasses, raises his hand and asks, "Did we lose?" to which I reply, "Do you feel like we lost?" To which he replies, sheepishly, "yes."

On my way out I'm confronted by a guy from the Grand Ledge Youth Football board of directors who wears aviator shades all the time and thinks he's Maverick from *Top Gun*. "That your team?" he asks, pointing in the direction of our practice field. "Tell them to stop sitting on their helmets."

Nice.

I text Kristin, "Horrible scrimmage." I know that she doesn't "get" the competitive animal that rages inside me when it comes to sports. She thinks my reaction to youth sports is ridiculous. For a man of culture and refinement (most days) to turn into a blathering rage-aholic in the event of a bad scrimmage is, indeed, ridiculous.

"What went bad about it?" she replies.

"We just couldn't do anything," I write. "We could barely complete a center/quarterback exchange."

"Well, what was the score?" she asks later, at home.

"It's a scrimmage so you don't keep score, but I guess if we had, we would have won," I explain.

I watch my wife's face and witness confusion billowing up inside her, yet she isn't saying anything. The silence just makes it worse. I decide to keep talking, which, as it turns out, is the wrong decision.

"Yeah, so we scored one touchdown. It was Tristan on a forty-yard run—and they didn't score any—"

She cuts me off.

"Our own *son* scored the winning touchdown, and you are still angry?"

She's now livid as well as confused. We "won" but I am angry because it feels like we "lost" because we played poorly. In my competitive economy, merely coming out ahead and having my son score on a dazzling forty-yard run isn't enough. "I hate that Tim gets to go home feeling like a winner because we couldn't move the ball and that I feel like a loser," I explain, thinking that if I just continue talking I'll say something sensible eventually. It doesn't work.

We coaches are in a constant, maniacal pursuit of perfection. We want to see the perfect play, run perfectly, in the perfect situation. We want to deploy the perfect defensive alignment. However, as Christians, we're called to live for Christ and have no other gods before Him, including the god of winning at everything. If football (or writing, or whatever) is my all, then I *have* to win, all the time, to stave off the agony of losing. This is, of course, impossible.

When it comes to football, I've always felt so competent and in control that I've never invited God to be a part of this particular area of my life. I've never confessed my football-related idolatries, and never expressed how deeply and constantly I need my Savior to redeem this coaching experience, and to bring goodness and joy out of it. I've never considered that God gives and takes away, and that He's no less good if He takes away victories, or even takes away my opportunities to play the game I love and that He gifted me to play.

SECRET, HEART-LEVEL SINS

Kristin can't understand why winning matters so much to me, and our challenge is to help me discern when my desire to win is okay and when it crosses the line into sin. It's sin when I have to have perfection. It's sin when my evening is ruined without it, and I take that frustration out on my wife and sons. It's sin because my insistence that everything be perfect wrecks my ability to be grateful for the things God *has* given me.

Of course, nobody (besides Kristin) knew how angry I was after the scrimmage because I shook Tim's hand and told him his team did a great job. Nor did anyone know when I had the same angry reaction recently when our neighborhood association sent a form letter asking me to "please paint the trim on your front porch" and "do something about the weeds in your yard and garden." I didn't just read the letter, reflect on it, and decide what to do about it. I wanted to punch someone in the face for suggesting that my house wasn't perfect and that I hadn't done a perfect job of caring for my family and my home. I was also aggravated because it was my idea to move into the kind of neighborhood where people are so uptight about such things.

Even though I'm not famous, I still want to be thought of as "great" and "successful." I want people to think that my books are extraordinary works of staggering genius. I want Grand Ledgers to think that I'm an amazing youth football coach. This is why scrimmage losses and three-star Amazon reviews of my books hurt so badly, because I have so much on the line (my ego, my reputation as a "winner"), even if it's only in my own sinful heart.

In *The Pursuit of God* A.W. Tozer called these "self-sins":

> *To be specific, the self-sins are self-righteousness, self-pity, self-confidence, self-sufficiency, self-admiration, self-love and a host of others like them. They dwell too deep within us and are too much a part of our natures to come to our attention till the light of God is focused upon them. The grosser manifestations of these sins—egotism, exhibitionism, self-promotion—are strangely tolerated in Christian leaders, even in circles of impeccable orthodoxy. They are so much in evidence as actually, for many people, to become identified with the gospel. . . . Promoting self under the guise of promoting Christ is currently so common as to excite little notice. . . .*
>
> *Let us beware of tinkering with our inner life, hoping ourselves to rend the veil. God must do everything for us. Our part is to yield and trust. We must confess, forsake, repudiate the self-life, and then reckon it crucified.*[2]

It's the yielding and trusting, of course, that is the hard part.

LOSING MY LIFE TO FIND IT

One day I explained all of this to a biblical counselor. Despite his gentleness and wisdom, he struggles in some of the same areas. He asked me to do a simple exercise, which was to reread Galatians 5:1-6, replacing the word *circumcision* with whatever word or phrase sums up the operative idol in my heart, be it perfection (or money or success).

> *It is for freedom that Christ has set us free. Stand firm, then, and do not let yourselves be burdened again by a yoke of slavery.*
>
> *Mark my words! I, Paul, tell you that if you let yourselves be [slaves to perfection], Christ will be of no value to you at all. Again, I declare to every man who lets himself be [enslaved to perfection] that he is obligated to obey the whole law. You who are trying to be justified by the law have been alienated from Christ; you have fallen away from grace. For through the Spirit we eagerly await by faith the righteousness for which we hope. For in Christ Jesus neither [perfection] or [lack of perfection] has any value. The only thing that counts is faith expressing itself through love.*

Try that exercise with your household god—be it perfection or winning or money or your children or your own sense of theological perfection. Think about the heartache of Christ being, as Paul writes, "of no value to you at all." Think about the futility of being "justified" by your success or your money or even the grandeur of your children. Allow Christ to be your all, or at least a little more of your all than He is currently. This exercise helps me walk down the path toward crucifying my own idols. It's not easy. I still want perfection from myself and others, but this passage helps me fight it. And it helps me to look to the only One who can be perfect for me.

"DO YOU STILL HAVE FAITH?"

In the previous passage Paul said that the only thing that counts is "faith expressing itself through love." What does faith look like in a context in which everything seems dark and hopeless?

Jesus gives us a glimpse in Mark 4:35-41, when He calms the storm. The text says that a "furious squall" came up and the waves were so high that the boat was "nearly swamped." The disciples must have feared for their lives, thinking they would be swallowed up by the dark storm and the angry waves. Through it all, Jesus slept. The disciples were (understandably) distraught and probably annoyed with Jesus. "Teacher, don't you care if we drown?" they asked. I know the feeling. I've been in that place; I've wondered if God even cared that I was drowning professionally, athletically, maritally, or otherwise. But He did, and He does.

The text says that Jesus got up and "rebuked the wind." This must have been a powerful moment, and we experience these moments in life when the storm abates and the clouds part and we can breathe again, knowing that our Lord has taken care of us. It's a moment in which we're reminded that we serve a faithful God who loves us. Jesus said, finally, to His disciples: "Why are you so afraid? Do you still have no faith?"

BECOMING "POOR IN SPIRIT"

We evidence our lack of faith when we expect an unreasonable amount of perfection from others.

"Last summer at a Little League softball game I watched a father publicly berate his hysterical son, not only for striking out, but for crying about it," wrote Cheryl Forbes in *The Religion of Power*. "The father's disgust and near-hatred were visible on his face for all of us to see, including his son. This man felt powerless because his son wasn't a great player, and the son felt powerless to gain his father's love and respect because he couldn't even make contact with the ball. This is a painful illusion of our refusal to allow failure in our children."[3]

This scenario is, of course, tragic. Written on a page it looks ridiculous for a father to demand perfection from his son. We would never say that we love our kids less because of something as trivial as their performance in a softball game (or football game). The answer to the problem of perfection isn't a society where everybody "wins," because kids, intuitively, still know who lost in the same way that their parents know. The answer isn't the sort of nanny-state, soft-focus culture in which every child gets a blue ribbon and is routinely lied to about how successful and talented he or she is. This is patronizing to children and just as stifling to their development, as it will create a sense of entitlement and disillusionment down the line that cannot be slaked.

The answer to the quest for perfection is a posture of meek humility and sober consciousness of our sinfulness that allows us to direct our gaze at Christ alone. When I'm meek, my gaze isn't directed at myself. I'm no longer looking to my own perfection—or my own victories, or my own good book reviews—to define me. I'm looking to the One who died on my behalf.

The first three verses of the Beatitudes in Matthew 5 focus on a particular posture of spirit:

Blessed are the poor in spirit,
for theirs is the kingdom of heaven.
Blessed are those who mourn,
for they will be comforted.
Blessed are the meek,
for they will inherit the earth.

This is a posture that emphasizes our own acknowledgment and brokenheartedness over the condition of our hearts. "Poor in spirit" doesn't mean "poor in bank account"; rather, it means the condition of soul poverty in which we are grieved over the ways in which we've sinned against our Lord.

When we mourn, we're mourning the condition of our hard hearts apart from Christ, like David does in Psalm 51:

Have mercy on me, O God,
according to your unfailing love;
according to your great compassion
blot out my transgressions.
Wash away all my iniquity
and cleanse me from my sin.

For I know my transgressions,
   and my sin is always before me.
Against you, you only, have I sinned
   and done what is evil in your sight;
so you are right in your verdict
   and justified when you judge.
Surely I was sinful at birth,
   sinful from the time my mother conceived me.
Yet you desired faithfulness even in the womb;
   you taught me wisdom in that secret place. (vv. 1-6)

Being meek doesn't mean being wan, pale, and passive.[4] It doesn't mean we don't compete. It just means that, in a spiritual sense, we don't defend ourselves—we don't always have to "win." When we are poor in spirit, we don't stand on our own rights because we have no rights to stand on. So, in the context of the Beatitudes, I *can't* go home from the game and defend my competitive rage to my wife. I can't say, "Well, that's just the way I am," nor can I say, "As a competitor I've been trained to hate losing." I can only grieve of my need to always win, repent of it, and cry out to God for a changed and clean heart, like David did.

FIGHTING THE FEAR OF IMPERFECTION

In my office next to my computer (subtext: I'm working on football stuff) is a sheet of notebook paper stuck on the side of some file drawers. On it, in Kristin's handwriting, are the words "Goals for Coaching," and the list includes things like

"Be salt and light—encourage hurting kids and parents," as well as "Look for opportunities to share the gospel." The final line under the "Ted" column reads, "Quell competitive rage."

There's the rub. The source of my rage about my imperfect performance is fear, and I've never been good at living without fear. I fear the reactions of the parents of the kids I coach, I fear ridicule in front of the board of directors, and I fear that my friends will think less of me if my team loses. I've been full of fear over the decisions I *have* made, and I've let fear paralyze me from making decisions and taking advantage of opportunities in life. It occurs to me that most of my household gods—wanting the absolute best for my wife, a pain-free life for my kids, and a sterling reputation—are all the fruits of fear.

And sometimes clinging to fear even makes me *appear* noble. After all, everyone admires a dad who wants the best for his wife and kids. Everyone admires a dad who works his tail off to provide a good life for his family.

But in light of Christ and His promises, what is there to fear?

Isaiah 41:10 reads, "So do not fear, for I am with you; do not be dismayed, for I am your God. I will strengthen you and help you; I will uphold you with my righteous right hand." We need to cling to that verse in moments of idolatry-related panic and fear. We are commanded not to fear and are also given the ultimate reason why Christians, if anyone, should enjoy fear-free lives: "For I am with you . . . for I am your God." We are then given the added promise that God will strengthen, help, and uphold us with His righteous right hand. When it comes to fleeing the household god of winning, we need to fight fear with faith. Faith that—win or lose—our God will uphold us with His righteous right hand.

Faith, in a nutshell, is the ability to *believe* in those promises when the chips are down. I pray that God would give me the grace to handle the upcoming day and would—despite all logic and reason—bring me *joy* in my interactions with kids and parents on our team.

DESIRE FOR HEAVEN ON EARTH

I've heard a lot lately about a concept I like to call "looking for heaven on earth." We want everything to be perfect, right now; we're frustrated with imperfections, big and small. We feel this way a lot. Even when things are mostly good, we think things like, *My marriage is going well, my kids are healthy, we're doing okay financially, our church is great . . . if only my job were more fulfilling.*

Or, *I've got a lot of friends, a job I love, I'm healthy and independent, if only I were married, then everything would be perfect.*

Or, *I've got great relationships with family and friends, I'm loved and respected, my life is rich and rewarding; why can't I just make some more/enough money?*

Or, *Last year we had plenty of money, but our marriage was struggling. This year our marriage is strong, but we can't make ends meet. Why is there always something?*

All of these thoughts reflect the same longing—why can't

things be perfect? I've got almost everything I want; why can't I have it all?

We are inherently greedy. Good is never good enough. Not until we've been through something really bad do we see how minor those little downers are. And even then, even when we have this higher perspective, it doesn't make us immune to still wanting everything to be working out for us.

To be sure, the things lacking are often significant things: we all need adequate amounts of money, love, health, and sense of purpose. It is true that life would be better, more enjoyable, if every aspect of our lives were on track at the same time—or better yet, all the time. But I think God could have a greater purpose in all this for us. If everything, here and now, were so great, would we care about heaven? Would we care about God? It is true that our hearts yearn for perfection, for things to be intrinsically right; this is the way God created us. Yet He Himself is that source of perfection and rightness that we ought to turn to. But we are so easily pacified with paltry substitutes! If all my ducks were in a row here and now, in the things I can see and experience, why would I look to the less immediately tangible (if more complete and everlasting) goodness found only in God? I wouldn't. I would revel in my worldly substitutions and be satisfied with second best. So I think God allows us to experience these niggling frustrations (even true tragedies, sometimes) to remind us that only heaven, with God, is truly heaven.

⇌ *From Kristin* ⇌

Everyone loves the Olympics. They bring out the patriotic best in everyone, watching all those bright-eyed hopefuls competing. And one of my favorite movies, *Chariots of Fire*, is about the Olympics. Granted, I love that movie mostly for the gorgeous 1920s fashion, and less for the sports element, but that's what makes a great movie great—its appeal on multiple levels.

So I ought to love the Olympics, just like everyone else, but I don't. I hate them. I can't watch them because the Olympics are about being perfect. There's the winner, and then there's everybody else. There is something about watching someone's dreams die that just makes me sick. We watch these athletes—every one of them world class, the absolute best in the world—compete, and all but three lose. Say there are several runners lined up across the track, all of them unbelievably fast. The gun goes off, they run like mad, and you need some ultra-precise, state-of-the-art stopwatch to even know who won. And then winners win by 1/100th of a second, often not even discernible to the naked eye. Which is super for the winner, but then there are a lot of runners who are crazy fast, faster than anyone else in the world, and they are losers. I can't stand it! I am a good American, and having lived some time in post-Soviet countries, I do not believe that communism works. But when it comes to the Olympics, a teeny little part of my commie side shows.

(Actually, that's not true—the communists were notably relentless in their pursuit of Olympic gold. Anyone who has seen *Rocky IV*[5] knows this.)

CHAPTER 7

Herod's Temple

THE HOUSEHOLD GOD OF BEING ONE OF THE "HAVES"

For a moment down there, you got that chip off your
shoulder (points to shoulder). You let people in.
— JERRY MAGUIRE TO ROD TIDWELL, IN *JERRY MAGUIRE*

Put to death, therefore, whatever belongs to your
earthly nature: sexual immorality, impurity, lust,
evil desires and greed, which is idolatry.
— COLOSSIANS 3:5

I'm dropping my kids off at the local megachurch for a week
of Vacation Bible School, which could be alternately named
The Thing You Do at the End of the Summer Because
Your Kids Are Driving You Crazy. I don't go to the local
megachurch. I go to a smallish congregation (two hundred
people?) that rents space in a local community center, and
it's been years since I've darkened the door of this particular
megachurch. In fact, I think the last time I was here it was to

play basketball on their NBA-practice-gym-quality floor in the main gym, as opposed to the youth gym.

Caveat: It's not especially noble to go to a small church. It's just that when you're walking through a Christian version of Herod's temple, it's hard not to think about the issues surrounding "having" and "not having." This church "has." Big time. It has teaching pastors, pastors that handle the business, associate pastors, youth pastors, associate youth pastors, shepherding pastors,[1] and family pastors. Jesus, with His insistence on poverty of spirit, would probably have a tough time landing a pastoral gig at one of these churches.

I was paralyzed by have-and-have-not issues when I was at Taylor—cognizant as I was that there were buildings on campus named after relatives of my classmates; cognizant as I was that were it not for football I had no business being there; cognizant as I was, for the first time, that it's a truism that money really *can* buy respect, and jobs, and opportunities.

I once even wrote about have-and-have-not issues in an open letter to my college's alumni magazine:

> *After ripping through the heavy plastic with a pair of common kitchen scissors, I especially enjoy the ultra-hi-res close-up shot of something quasi-spiritual on the cover—things like clay (see also: the potter, and His), sand (see also: what not to build your house upon, see also: the foolish man), a rock (see also: what the wise man built his house upon), and sheet metal (see also: ???).*
>
> *I'm also comforted to see that, for the most part, the*

students who were affluent, attractive, and popular
when I was in school have remained so, as evidenced
by their pictures in your magazine. That's good. I'm
often afraid of what will become of kids from amazing
families, with tons of money, great cars, nice hair, and
every other advantage known to man. Good to see
they're not slipping through the cracks somehow.

Finally, it's especially gratifying to see my classmates
out-awesome-ing each other via the short alumni
updates in the back. I'm comforted to see how amazing
everyone's family and job is. (For the next issue: My
family and job are both awesome. Class of 1998).[2]

I don't think it's a stretch to say that most people in the
Christian entertainment business started out as "haves" and
will probably end up as haves. When you're a have-not, it's
just too hard to make it. There's no money for writer's conferences, or studio space to record your record, or trips to LA
to pitch your culture-engaging screenplay. No trust fund.
No rich uncle. No safety net. No going back to school for
another degree when you realize the first one wasn't fulfilling.
When you're a have-not, you do what you have to do to get
by and, thus, there are many have-nots who never get the
opportunity to do their thing.

Admission: My wife is a caterer. She was approached by
someone on behalf of the local megachurch about a cater-
ing gig. Essentially the church wanted a gourmet meal but
wanted it for free because of how nice and meaningful their

ministry is. Kristin, of course, couldn't take the job because working for free isn't, generally, good business. This experience only muddies the waters for our family and picks at the "money issues" scab. I'm cynical about this, and it's sinful to be cynical. Please forgive me for that—and I mean that. God is, and has always been, sovereign over the haves and the have-nots. I know this with my head and need to feel and believe it in my heart and soul.

As I walk my fifth grader down the carpeted hallways of the megachurch, past the suite of offices, past the play area outside that looks like Noah's ark minus the Flood that wiped out all of humankind because of humanity's rampant and unchecked sinfulness, past the café complete with exposed brick and ductwork because in the late nineties exposed brick and ductwork was focus-grouped as "cool," and finally past a Lollapalooza-quality soundstage earmarked for use by the "youth," I'm struck with the following thought: *Money is literally growing on the fake ficus trees in here, yet at the same time two of my best friends are passionate, sincere, intellectual, gospel-preaching pastors at small churches that are perpetually going broke and are perpetually at risk of dying. These men* love *the Word and pray for their parishioners. Lord, why the inequity? And what's more, why is this megachurch even here? What are we "winning" people to when we win them with a church that looks like a cross between a Chuck E. Cheese's franchise (albeit a very clean one) circa 1997, the MGM Grand, and Sandals Jamaica?*

The reductive answer is that people like nice things. This has been the case since the beginning of time. A more interesting answer is that people, and families in particular, crave *comfort*, and a church like this is nothing if not, at some level, a shrine to comfort. Comfort is everywhere here. From the chaise lounges in the youth room, to the leather sofas in the lobbies, to the climate-control heating and cooling systems, to the taupe color scheme that makes the sanctuary look like a gigantic version of your mother-in-law's sitting room. Comfort is king.

CHRISTIANITY THAT'S "WORKING"

A church like this is, at a subconscious level, selling the idea that "although your life may be uncertain and even in turmoil, you can experience a slice of heaven here every Sunday morning and Wednesday night, so sit back and enjoy the show. We also have lattes." The message is that even if you're not doing okay, you'll at least feel like you're doing well here.

"We like knowing that famous and beautiful people are Christians; it makes us average Christians seem that much more important," wrote Cheryl Forbes in *The Religion of Power* some thirty-plus years ago. "But the ugly, the maimed, the poor, the weak, the untalented? What about the God Man in whom there was no beauty? Jesus had no influence, riches, or power. He was in human terms a loser. No, we can't project that image: And image is all. Who would buy our product without the right packaging? Would we have bought it in the first place? Unless Christianity works, what good is it?"[3]

Many—including, at times, me and my family—believe that Christianity "working" means that we're comfortable, we have enough money, and everyone in the family is healthy and happy.

I can see the gears turning in my fifth-grade son's mind: *Foosball, billiards, Xboxes, flat-screens, a climbing wall, a soundstage, leather sofas everywhere . . . why doesn't* our *church look like this?* I don't blame him. I love/hate this place. It reminds me of the chip that still, occasionally, resides right here (points to shoulder). It's a chip I thought I had unloaded, but that comes back occasionally.

I resent these khaki-wearing, perma-grinned people for their apparent abundance of comfort, but the thing is, I want it too. I don't necessarily want a church with a flat-screen television every ten paces, but I want *comfort* for my family. I want my wife to not have to work. I want my kids to have new shoes whenever they need them. I want to be able to take my wife on a nice trip periodically.

THE GOD OF ALL COMFORT (AND DISCOMFORT)

After dropping off my son, I walk the half mile back through the building toward the lobby, toward the acres-worth of parking lot. As I walk, I grapple with the following questions: How do I feel about a God who keeps me in a perpetual state of financial discomfort? And how do I feel about a God who may take away something I really want?

I don't have to look too deeply into Scripture to find people who were taken care of, comforted, and even joyful in the face of loads of discomfort. There's Joseph in prison. Paul in prison. Daniel in the lions' den. David on the lam and fearing for his life. David crying out to God for a clean heart, and then receiving one. Abraham and Sarah in infertility.

It's possible. We flee the idol of being one of the "haves" when we don't turn our backs on the God who, sovereignly, keeps us in discomfort for a season. We trust Him in the discomfort. We confess sin when there is sin to be confessed.

There are other examples of people who chose comfort over trusting the God of the universe to meet their needs. The rich, young ruler, when faced with the decision of a lifetime, chose comfort. Luke 18:18-25 reads:

> *A certain ruler asked him, "Good teacher, what must I do to inherit eternal life?"*
>
> *"Why do you call me good?" Jesus answered.*
> *"No one is good—except God alone. You know the commandments: 'You shall not commit adultery, you shall not murder, you shall not steal, you shall not give false testimony, honor your father and mother.'"*
>
> *"All these I have kept since I was a boy," he said.*
>
> *When Jesus heard this, he said to him, "You still lack one thing. Sell everything you have and give to the poor, and you will have treasure in heaven. Then come, follow me."*
>
> *When he heard this, he became very sad, because he was very wealthy. Jesus looked at him and said, "How hard it is for the rich to enter the kingdom of God! Indeed, it is easier for a camel to go through the eye of a needle than for someone who is rich to enter the kingdom of God."*

Is there is something of the Rich, Young Ruler in me? Are there things I'm not willing to give up? Perhaps on a heart level, I'm unwilling to give up small luxuries such as being able to buy new shoes for my kids at the beginning of the school year. Perhaps I'm unwilling to give up being perceived as a quote/unquote good provider for my family. The Rich, Young Ruler was unable to give up his own glory for the promise of God's glory. What am I unwilling to give up? Being a writer? Having a cool career? Having a "life of the body" (athletics) as well as a "life of the mind"? Perhaps I need God to strip me of these things in order to fully rely on Him, in order to fully experience His glory.

In my experience, I don't even have what it takes to begin dethroning this idol. God is doing it for me. By sometimes allowing me to be in a state of financial distress, He is keeping me reliant on Him. Because I want nice things too much, and too often, I don't have the strength within myself to choose otherwise. God has to do it for me.

Because I have different tastes, I find it easy to disdain and turn away from the local megachurch. *That's an indulgence for a different kind of person*, I think to myself. But am I really any different?

⇆ *From Kristin* ⇆

I love comfort. For me, comfort is: great food, attractive surroundings, plenty of sleep and leisure time, and pretty clothes. It's also being well-liked, having enough money so decisions aren't made based on how much stuff costs, and being with the people I like. Your ideas of comfort may be different, but you get the idea—comfort is whatever makes you feel good.

And like all the other idols we've discussed in the book, it's not inherently evil. God fills our lives with blessings and good things (Psalm 107:9), and we can enjoy those things and thank Him for them. So when does comfort become an idol of the heart, something we cherish above God Himself? For me, every single day. Every time I decide to cut short tucking my kids in because I want to hurry on to relaxing. Every time I mentally glare at God for allowing trouble when I want ease and good times. Every time my day is ruined because my food is subpar. (This happens. Embarrassingly often.) Every time I get skeezed out by a person based on his or her surroundings or appearance. Every time I am ungracious to people because they've hurt me or I don't like them. These are all examples of putting my comfort, my likes, ahead of what's right to do.

Comfort within the family is tricky. Our family, our homes, are supposed to be our haven and our place of rest, so it's only natural that we want them to be comfortable—both in the sense of physical comfort (pleasant temperature, safe, cozy) and in the sense of the way we like it. But what about when my definition of comfort clashes with another family member's definition? For example, some people are (inexplicably) animal lovers. No home is a home without a friendly, furry presence there—or so I hear. Because I am, most decidedly, not an animal lover. Not only do animals not excite me, they positively repel me—dirt, odors, saliva, shedding, untoilet trained—what is there to like?

But what about all the other preferences, like my desire for neatness, order, and quiet to reign in my home? These fly directly in the face of my children's utter determination to bring the noise, bring the funk. As a parent I do have a right to lay down some rules for our home, and most of the comfort issues are not moral issues, so I have some freedom in Christ. But I do need to take care that my love of comfort is not ruling the day at the expense of everyone else. I can make decisions that impact my home life with sense (it's good for my kids to learn how to live quietly and neatly) and with some eye to my own comfort, but I need to be sure that comfort doesn't own me.

I need to make sure comfort doesn't own me in a spiritual sense either. If I'm not careful, I can begin to make every decision in my life through the lens of my comfort. And before long, I've created a version of God who exists only to meet my needs and make me happy. A God who exists only to justify my decisions. And this is not God's chief end.

CHAPTER 8

Does God Love Me or Is He a Cosmic Trickster?

THE HOUSEHOLD GOD OF CYNICISM AND IRONY

Hope deferred makes the heart sick.
— PROVERBS 13:12

It's the last day of VBS, and we've just dropped our kids at the megachurch with Noah's ark and the flat-screen TVs one last time. We're wheeling our way out of the well-heeled suburbs, through the truly crummy ghetto part of Lansing, through the gentrified-hipster-coffee-shop part of Lansing, and into an industrial area that is home to a tiny, wonderful breakfast place called Golden Harvest, which sits across the street from a lumberyard.

Golden Harvest has something of a reputation in the Lansing area, as it is known for making the best pancakes and waffles in the Midwest and is located in an area informally known to be a place to score pot. It's a tiny space, with no more than fifteen tables, so patrons are often required to wait outside until they're called in by the owner and seated. Loud techno, punk, or hip-hop music is always throbbing out the front door, and the patrons outside are always either: (a) hipsters, (b) regulars, (c) cops, which is weird given the second half of Golden H's local rep, or (d) mortified-looking people who read about it on Yelp but didn't know that Golden Harvest is the *least* family-friendly breakfast place in the history of breakfast places.

Warning, Hipster Arrogance Ahead: Our family is friendly with the owner. This makes us feel cool, unabashedly. She waves us inside and comments that it's been a long time since we've been in. We tell her that our kids are at VBS and it's the last free morning we'll have until school starts. Her husband is behind the counter making magic on the grill. Her girls—homeschooled, not in the evangelical way but rather in the ultimate libertarian/anarchist way—are starring on a youth Roller Derby team.[1]

Kristin and I are in a celebratory mood. We've looked into the dark heart of our finances and found that we do indeed have the money to go to France, where I've been given the opportunity to play and coach American football. This is an experience we've wanted for a long time, and about which we say things like "once in a lifetime" as we try to justify the trip to each other. The thought of being in France has me giddy with excitement, and we're sitting at the Formica table, guzzling coffee, shouting at each other over Bassnectar, and planning all the creative genius that France is going to inspire.

We prayed on the way to breakfast. We prayed that God

would make it *clear* whether we should book the France tickets. We prayed that He would encourage us that morning, as looking at finances often has the opposite effect.[2] He appears to be doing just that: when I ask the owner about the check, she explains that she's taken care of it, and we drive home thrilled, filled, and thankful for God and the Golden H.

Back at home, our plan is to fire up the laptops and purchase our plane tickets. We've been checking travel sites like Kayak.com furiously, trying to mastermind the best possible time and way in which to book our tickets. Today, we've decided, is the day.

"Let me just check our accounts one more time before we buy," says Kristin, rummaging through the piles of paper on her little desk. We're continually buying little mid-century-mod trinkets and baskets for her to "organize her desk" and "put receipts in." It never works. The desk, and our finances, remain a mess. I wait.

Finally she comes into my office, crestfallen. "We're shorter than I thought," she explains, shuffling some papers in her hands. I can tell she's afraid to tell me how much.

"How much?" I reply, expecting her to have misplaced $500 or $1,000 in some business or health savings account someplace. I am prepared to pat her on the shoulder and be the calm, good-natured, comforting guy that I am trying, in Christ, to sometimes be.

"We're short $10,000," she says. I am silent. I am not the good-natured, comforting, roll-with-it guy. I am the opposite of that guy. I see France slipping away. I can't, in good faith, go to the computer and spend several thousand dollars on the selfsame wild, carefree, creative adventure that we had been dreaming about and celebrating just minutes before at Golden Harvest.

Kristin feels awful about her mistake and apologizes profusely. "It's not your fault," I reply. I mean it *is* her fault in the sense that she misplaced *ten thousand dollars*, but it's not her fault that we don't have the money. I spiral into a self-indulgent fit of self-pity and cynicism, which, incidentally, I have been trying for the last two years to crucify. It's the kind of cynicism, in a nutshell, that says, "Stuff like this always happens to me." I shut off the lights and just lie, silently, in bed, waiting for something good to happen.

I should clarify that by saying she *misplaced* the money, I do not mean Kristin left it folded in a newspaper on a counter for our evil nemesis to discover, à la Uncle Billy from *It's a Wonderful Life*. She thought she had tucked it into the savings account to await the purchase of our tickets to France, but instead put it into our checking account, where we spent it paying the mortgage, buying groceries, and eating chorizo burritos and French toast at Golden Harvest.

KNOW YOUR ENEMY

Cynicism, which *A Praying Life* author Paul Miller describes as the absence of hope, has been my personal sin/cross to bear for most of my life. Cynicism, or expecting things to go badly so that I'm not surprised/disappointed when they do, has been my main defense mechanism since, oh, middle school. It's manifested itself sometimes in humor, sometimes in anger, sometimes in just hardened silence. Like today.

When I was freelancing for ESPN in the early 2000s, my cynicism served me well. Snarky, ironic stories brought positive reactions from editors and laughs from audiences who, by that time, had become so steeped in detached irony that hope and earnestness seemed a thousand miles away. My generation (Generation X, the nineties, and so on) seemed to invent sarcasm, and like many others, I reveled in the gift of it. There was nothing a raised eyebrow and a jaded, ironic snicker couldn't fix. As long as I had sarcasm I didn't have to worry about dashed hopes, because hope was for suckers.

Today my cynicism is born of the disappointment that comes with *not* providing quite enough for my family. I am realizing, anew, that I'm *not* qualified to be an idol to my wife and kids. I am *not* their ultimate provider. I feel that I hoped in vain for the trip to France and am now paying the price for hoping. I sense the disappointment that is coming for them and feel that the only thing I've been consistent at providing is, in fact, disappointment.

Cynicism, ultimately, is a patent, gut-level distrust of God's essential goodness. The Bible says over and over again that God is good. God is our fortress. God is our stronghold. God is our deliverer. God delights in giving us good things.

The world, to a cynic, suggests otherwise. The world suggests that God is a crusher of dreams, a denier of appetites, and a cosmic trickster. Today I am tempted to believe just that—that God shows me something good and then takes it away. Cynicism keeps hope at arm's length. It's a form of self-protection. If I'm never hopeful, I'll never be disappointed.

Can I still trust?

"Don't get cynical," Kristin says. "Don't be the old you." It's a scriptural word of encouragement. She is parroting something that she's heard me say, which is that I don't want to be the "old me." The me who had a wisecrack and a sneer and a defeatist attitude that denied God's essential goodness. She is imploring me to not take my God-given, Cross-purchased heart of flesh and replace it again, even momentarily, with a heart of stone.

But it's tempting to see our France experience slipping away and not do exactly that.

BEATING CYNICISM

I may never beat cynicism. But I'm required, as I am with all sins, to fight against it, and to fight hard, and to keep fighting. To do this, I need the help of my friends and family. I need them to preach the gospel to me when I'm too weary and defeated to do it myself. They don't do this with greeting card platitudes; they do it by mourning with me when I mourn, and by gently reminding me that I serve a God who has seen me through trials in the past and will see me through the trial I'm in.

I also need to fight cynicism with thankfulness. Sometimes this process is excruciating. After reading the bad review or seeing the dwindling bank account, thanking God for what I *do* have can feel counterintuitive. But I must. I must remember all that God has done for me and thank Him for His goodness. I need to trust that "I will see the goodness of the LORD in the land of the living."[3]

Finally, I need to remember who I serve. Matthew 7:9-11 reads, "Which of you, if your son asks for bread, will give him a stone? Or if he asks for a fish, will give him a snake? If you, then, though you are evil, know how to give good gifts to your children, how much more will your Father in heaven give good gifts to those who ask him!"

Despite my cynicism, I still know how to give good gifts to my children. I still love seeing their faces light up when they rip into a package. I still love surprising them. As a child of God, I can't lose the ability to be surprised by grace. I can't let cynicism harden me to that degree. I can't be so hard (or scared) that I stop asking my Father for good gifts—circumstantial gifts, and the gift of a changed heart.

And I have to remember that Christ died for my cynicism. Romans 8:1-4 reads, "Therefore, there is now no condemnation for those who are in Christ Jesus, because through Christ Jesus the law of the Spirit who gives life has set you free from the law of sin and death. For what the law was powerless to do because it was weakened by the flesh, God did by sending his own Son in the likeness of sinful flesh to be a sin offering. And so he condemned sin in the flesh, in order that the righteous requirement of the law might be fully met in us, who do not live according to the flesh but according to the Spirit."

It's only in Christ, and only at the Cross, that I can be free from cynicism. And be freed to hope again.

⇜ From Kristin ⇝

Of late we've seen a parade of rainbows. We've seen thick, short rainbows, double rainbows, vibrantly colored rainbows, full-bowed rainbows; we even thought we could see the place on the ground where the rainbow rested. I find it interesting that so many rainbows would appear to us right in the midst of a time when so much in our life is uncertain, and anxiety threatens to rise up and choke us.

Everybody knows that rainbows can be scientifically explained by the raindrops acting as a prism for the sunlight. But there is so much more to it than that when you remember that the rainbow is a visible sign of God's faithfulness to His children. He said so! Specifically, of course, He gave us rainbows to remind us that He won't flood the whole earth again. But I think rainbows mean so much more: That He doesn't change, ever. That He always keeps His promises. That He is faithful and true. So I don't think it is an accident that these rainbows would be popping up all over the place, right at this time in our lives. God can make a rainbow anytime, anyplace, and He certainly could have filled the sky with these tangible reminders of His faithfulness at home. But being placed here in France, in this place where they are so frequent, adds another layer of amazement to His ability to reveal Himself to us, if we have eyes to see. He is all around us, personal, involved, when we only take the time to see Him.

CHAPTER 9

Love Me, Love Me, Say That You Love Me

THE HOUSEHOLD GOD OF IMPRESSING OTHERS

The only true currency in this bankrupt world is what
you share with someone else when you're uncool.
— LESTER BANGS IN *ALMOST FAMOUS*

Things are good here. Teaching is going well. And I'm
playing the best tennis of my life. Maybe that's an
illusion, but . . . it feels that way.
— BERNARD BERKMAN IN *THE SQUID AND THE WHALE*

A friend of mine told the story of her father once sitting her
down and walking her through, page by page, a carefully
rendered photo album of each car he'd ever owned. Her dad
grew up in Detroit in the 1960s, when cars were central to
the culture of the time and place. Men worked in industries
that revolved around the car, and the car was the outward
symbol of a man's ability to provide. Her father's intention-
ality re: sitting her down and showing her his old cars was

his way of reaching out and letting her into his life. While he did not share stories about disappointment and longing and unrequited desires, he did show her pictures of a meticulously cared-for yellow 1965 Ford Mustang, allowing her to fill in the details on her own.

Interestingly, in the evangelical circles I frequent "providing" is a central theme. The Young Reformed Man sires lots of children,[1] and his primary source of pride/worth/status is often in how well he provides for said family. This isn't necessarily a bad thing. The Bible is clear that men need to provide for their families, but it's something that, culturally, we're allowed to be a little smug and self-satisfied about if it's going well. We're allowed to spend a few too many hours in the office and to be a little disconnected from the day-to-day details of our kids because it's the father's job to quote/unquote provide and it's the mother's job to know the kids, educate the kids, and worry about the kids. This is the role that she is allowed to be a little smug and self-congratulatory about.

For almost a decade, my means of providing for our family has been writing—specifically books. Many people (mistakenly) think that my professional life is a nonstop thrill ride of money, fame, and brushes with famous people—and I was more than happy to let them think that for a long time. Then one day Amazon.com—from whom you buy, well, nearly everything—decided to not only rank how well authors' individual books were selling, but also to rank *us* as authors in general. So now, saleswise, I can find out exactly how I'm doing compared to other authors. Needless to say, when I saw my ranking I freaked out—because it shattered my ability to impress others and impress myself. I wrote this letter to Amazon, in response:

Dear Amazon Author Rank (Beta),

I appreciate the e-mail this morning, alerting me to the fact that I am the 18,704th most popular author on all of Amazon.com, not to mention the 2013th most popular in the "Religion and Spirituality" category. You really know how to make a guy feel good about himself.

When I walk out the door each day to see that my neighbor's SUV seems to have grown larger and more magnificent overnight, or I have to go to a family function and listen to stories about cottage acquisitions, condos in Florida, cruises taken, or new cars purchased, I'll remember your e-mail with fondness. All I have to do to get a tangible sense for how I'm measuring up in this world is to look at the handy graph you've provided that charts my progress as an artist (updated hourly). If only Ernest Hemingway and Sylvia Plath had one of these when they were around! I bet their careers would have been a lot more joyful, and I bet they would have been a lot less depressed. I bet Ernest Hemingway would have checked his Amazon.com Author Central Page daily . . . updating his profile picture and smiling at the upward trajectory of his line graph. Thank you, Amazon.com.

*As the 18,704th most popular of your authors—
I know this comes with some clout but don't worry, I
put my pants on one leg at a time just like you—may
I humbly suggest some other rankings that would be
helpful in my life? Perhaps your algorithms can help in
the following areas:*

- **Amazon.com Tallness Ranking.** *I'd like to
  know, definitively, how my height measures
  up to that of other popular authors. Am
  I taller than Stephen King? How about the
  lanky but still elegant Garrison Keillor?*
- **Amazon.com Body Mass Index.** *Yeah,
  we're selling books, but are we staying fit?
  I mean sure, we can't buy sugar in New York
  City anymore, but what about the rest of us?*
- **Amazon.com Ranking of Who Makes the
  Most Money.** *This one is self-explanatory.
  Get on it, posthaste.*
- **Amazon.com Ranking of Which Authors
  Were the Best Athletes in High School.**
  *This one may be a little self-serving, but
  still . . . don't they say this is, quote, The Best
  Time of Our Lives? Let's QUANTIFY it!
  I mean, really, how much of a contributor
  was Joyce Carol Oates on her high school
  volleyball team?*

Well, I've put a lot on your already full plate, Amazon.com. No rush on any of that. Just know that I speak for artists everywhere when I say that it's a privilege to be able to check our rankings hourly. I can only imagine how Picasso and Renoir would have been helped by something like this. Oh, the possibilities. If only you could somehow link my line graph to those other postmodern barometers of Success in Life— Facebook and Twitter. Then all my "friends" and "followers" could see how well I'm really doing.

Appreciatively,
Ted Kluck
18,704th Most Popular [2]

THE TEMPTATION TO CREATE A SUCCESSFUL PERSONA

Now, today's Christians would never, in our current church context, show off our Amazon Author Rank or car collection as a tangible symbol of how well we've done. To do so would appear a little too obviously arrogant. It would have the appearance of shallowness. So instead we look to our online following to speak to our success. Or perhaps to our number of Facebook friends or to the size of our congregations.

Again, we would never say such things out loud. We would never say, "I define my own self-worth by the size of my Twitter following and the regularity with which people 'like' or 'retweet' what I'm saying." However, this may be operatively how we're living.

Social media is nothing if not an opportunity to do our "acts of righteousness" before men. The folders and folders worth of pictures of us surrounded by scores of needy third-world children,[3] the links to all of the causes we champion because we're so good-hearted, and even the links to good things such as sermons and quotes are done mostly, I would argue, under the auspices of getting "likes" or "retweets." We want the buzz. We want the little hit of endorphins that comes from knowing that we're *liked*. And in today's culture, the pursuit of being liked is often our operative God. Social media is the first thing we look at in the morning. We roll over, wipe the sleep out of our eyes, and grab our iPhones to see who has "liked" or commented on our posts.

For those of us in Christian entertainment, the self-promotional social media waters are even murkier. We're breathlessly urged by consultants and publicists to "grow our platform!" and "get our names out there!" Writing conferences that used to be about writing are now almost exclusively about marketing and promotion because, sadly, getting published isn't about writing as much as it is about how many people you know who could potentially promote and/or purchase your book. It's about moving product.

It seems to me, though, that Jesus had a lot to say about these motivations. In Matthew 6:2, He said, "When you give to the needy, do not announce it with trumpets, as the hypocrites do in the synagogues and on the streets, to be honored by others."

What is social media if not our culture's answer to

announcing things with trumpets? What is it if not a constant, low-level cry to be loved and affirmed by others?[4] Jesus goes on to say, about this sort of public spiritual showboating, that what we get from men and women will be the totality of our reward.[5] Matthew 6:2-4 reads, "Truly I tell you, they have received their reward in full. But when you give to the needy, do not let your left hand know what your right hand is doing, so that your giving may be in secret. Then your Father, who sees what you have done in secret, will reward you."

REMOVING THE SOCIAL MEDIA IDOL

Social media is a fickle master. In my experience, social media is like money; I need progressively *more* of it, just to be satisfied. I need more likes and more comments on my pictures and cleverness. I need another message in my inbox. I need more friends or followers.

I know this isn't a spiritual issue for everyone, but it was and is a spiritual issue for me.

How do I fight this? I fought it, initially, by pulling back from social media. This is something you might try if you struggle with this idol. It feels strange, at first. You reach for your phone to instinctively check Twitter, Facebook, and your blog. Then you realize you don't have them anymore. Initially this might be a little terrifying—realizing that posts are made, arguments are had, and moments are archived without you. Then you might realize you don't care.

I also fight it by realizing that envy and jealousy are at the heart of the social media experience. I want others to envy me by crafting my perfect online persona, and I, in turn, envy others for what they're promoting online. Proverbs 14:30 reads, "A heart at peace gives life to the body, but envy rots the bones." I want, and pray for, a heart at peace. First Corinthians 3:3 says, of jealousy and quarreling, "You are still worldly. For since there is jealousy and quarreling among you, are you not worldly? Are you not acting like mere humans?" The blogosphere (even the evangelical blogosphere) is nothing if not an incubator for jealousy and quarreling. There is, indeed, a place for taking stands (even online), but most of us need to guard our hearts when we go there, lest we become hardened and embittered by the experience.

I wonder if we don't take envy seriously enough as we battle the sin in our lives. In Galatians 5, *envy* is listed right alongside things like *witchcraft*, *drunkenness*, and *orgies*. James 3:14-15 says, finally, "But if you harbor bitter envy and self-ish ambition in your hearts, do not boast about it or deny the truth. Such 'wisdom' does not come down from heaven but is earthly, unspiritual, demonic."

I have harbored bitter envy and selfish ambition—even toward my friends and some of the people in my life who are closest to me. My industry makes it hard not to at times, but still, the problem starts in my heart. It's not exactly cutting off my hand or gouging out my eye, but stepping back from social media helped me fight this household god.

Eventually you might realize that you like the real people in your life (and even your family) more, now that you're not exposed to their online personas during every waking moment of your day. Then, eventually, you'll realize you're not living your life in light of how you'll photograph it and frame it on Facebook.

LOVE ME

Even in this book, I'm tempted to get you to think certain things about me. I could paint a picture of myself as a talented, fun-loving bohemian with a really cool career, a better-than-average athletic sidelife, two cool and attractive kids, and a talented and interesting wife. You may think about me, *Wow, Kluck really has it together inasmuch as he's met a lot of famous people, interacted with pro athletes, gets to pursue his passion for a living, and has a great and supportive family.*

That would all be somewhat true. I could write about all the charming and thoughtful ways in which I've reached out to my wife in order to encourage her, and the hours I've spent "shoulder to shoulder"[6] "doing life"[7] with my kids, and also the underprivileged people I've spent time quote/unquote discipling since I've been an adult. I could write funny vignettes that cleverly masquerade as self-deprecation but that really serve a greater purpose of glorifying *me* and making me look awesome. I could write all of this in such a way as to make my female readers say "aww" and my male readers thoughtfully say things like, "I'm really challenged by that"—the subtext of which would read, "I'm really jealous of that."

I could do that. I'm still the kind of person who wants

people to fall in love with the *image* of me. The clever writer. Athlete. Cool professor. Romantic husband. Involved dad. Super Christian.

However, I could also write that I barely have any online presence anymore[8] because I had to drop out of social media due to the sins of heart and actions that I committed when I *did* have an online presence. I could also write about how egotistically and hungrily I used to check my social media for comments, and how often I check my Amazon Author Rank.[9] I could write about how I went looking for people who would worship me and how pathetic and self-serving that was.

I could write that my sins of heart and action have done significant heart-level damage to some of the people who are closest to me in this world, and that it's *only* by the grace of God that I have a shot at having any kind of relationship with those people in perpetuity.

I could write that my Very Cool Career has, in fact, never made us enough money and that we bought a little too much house several years ago and may in fact foreclose on that house, which (foreclosure) feels like an Evangelical Scarlet Letter of epic, Dave Ramsey[10]-disappointing proportions. I could write about how, in order to make ends meet, I had to send my wife back to work (see: scarlet letters: evangelical) and have taken day laborer jobs grinding concrete and unloading airplanes in the middle of the night.

I've spent most of my professional life crafting a persona. Writers are all about the subtle and often subconscious work of crafting a "likable" and "believable" narrator. If we're not careful, that process of creating the most appealing narrator can bleed over into our regular lives such that we're almost always crafting and shaping and tweaking our personas for maximum effect.

In a way, social media has made everyone a writer of sorts, so in a way everyone is always crafting his or her persona. Ask any college kid with a computer and Facebook or Instagram account.

Americans are big on justifying our existence to others. We're big on the update letters that subtly or not-so-subtly trumpet our achievements. We're big on letting people know that if we took an afternoon to go to the beach because it was sunny, we worked overtime the next day to make up for it. In this, and in countless other ways, we live our lives for the benefit of those who are watching us.

THE PROBLEM WITH EGO

The problem with ego is that it is a master that cannot be satisfied. It's a thirst that can never be slaked. I can never quite feel good *enough* about myself based on accomplishments, how well I provide for my family, my bank account, or even the achievements of my kids.

Regardless of my circumstance, I must always remember who I am in Christ. Ephesians 1:4-8 reminds us:

> *For he chose us in him before the creation of the world to be holy and blameless in his sight. In love he predestined us for adoption to sonship through Jesus*

Christ, in accordance with his pleasure and will—to the praise of his glorious grace, which he has freely given us in the One he loves. In him we have redemption through his blood, the forgiveness of sins, in accordance with the riches of God's grace that he lavished on us.

That one small paragraph reminds me that I am chosen by God, adopted by God, and a recipient of God's glorious grace—through no effort of my own. I am forgiven by God, and I am to be the recipient of His lavish grace. I don't always acknowledge the receipt, and I don't always understand His ways, but I know that if I am in Christ, He will bestow wisdom, understanding, and grace.

WHOEVER LOSES THEIR PERSONA WILL FIND IT

For the first time in my life, I'm ambivalent about my own persona. I'm too old to see myself as a football player. I've written too many books to see myself as a hot, new, up-and-coming literary voice. I've taught for too many years in college and university settings to idealize the academic life. I enjoy each of these things; it's just that I no longer dream about any of them, which is a strange feeling. Perhaps God has finally stripped me of my vocational and athletic dreams so that I can serve Him precisely where He wants me. This is an exciting, but scary, place to be. Not having any dreams is scary, but my prayer is that it's where God wants me. Maybe you can relate.

Is there something that God is calling you to give up?

Perhaps you're experiencing a humbling professional circumstance . . . perhaps your kids embarrass you . . . or perhaps, for the first time, you're just feeling a lack of dreams and ambition. It may be exactly where God wants you to be. Trust Him.

↪ *From Kristin* ↩

Boy, this is a big one for me. I want, so badly, to be liked. By everyone. Even people I don't like. And not just liked: I want to be adored, respected, looked up to, imitated, and made to be the center of attention. For how I look, what I say, who I am, what I do, and how I cook. For my intelligence, my honesty, my kindness, my parenting, my spirituality, my creativity, my wit—even when these descriptions can't possibly apply to me. So much of what I do is filtered through the sieve of how it would appear to others. Sometimes this can be good—I might refrain from yelling at my kids, not because it's the wrong thing to do, but because there are other people around. I would never exercise or show any restraint with dessert if it wasn't for the fact that I care about my appearance (merely "being healthy" is not enough for me!). I've often wondered why women who are already skinny say they want to start exercising—what is the point if you already look good?

So much of what I do (consciously or not) for others' benefit is negative. I remember when I was in high school being asked to pray for the class. (I went to a Christian school; I'm not that old! And it's very important to me that you don't think of me as "that old.") Afterward, one of my friends told me I sounded funny when I prayed. I was using my "prayer voice." That's just a little thing, but indicative of the way we spin ourselves to suit the occasion. Sure, there are many different facets to our persons. We are created to be multidimensional, but yet we so often put our best foot forward in a way that is not entirely aboveboard, that could be hypocritical.

Aside from the inauthenticity angle, our desire, our need to impress others can be deadly. Because so often impressing others causes us to turn away from choices God wants us to make. At the very least, it causes us to take our focus away from pleasing God and put it on pleasing people. The idol is valuing others' opinions over God's opinion. And it's so insidious! What's wrong with just wanting to be nice, to be liked? We live in a society, after all, and we have to interact with each other, so we might as well be pleasant. And that is true, but when impressing others is your idol, you do not want to be pleasant for others' benefit, you want to be pleasant so they will like you. And when you place being liked as top priority, you can do a lot of damage. Like making a joke at someone else's expense so you can earn a few guffaws. Or making a damaging decision to go along with the crowd (it may come as a surprise, but this temptation extends far beyond high school).

It can be confusing, but people pleasing is way more about me than it is about others. It's putting myself on the pedestal that only God should be on. It can seem like it's others-centered, but it's actually me-centered. I am acting in a certain way in order to get people to feel positively about me. Kind of like the trap of service, and how there is no true altruism; even when we are serving others, we are hoping to get a hit of good feelings from it.

CHAPTER 10

You've Gotta See My Book

THE HOUSEHOLD GOD OF GETTING PUBLISHED

What is it about high school? You read all the worst
books by good writers.

— BERNARD BERKMAN IN *THE SQUID AND THE WHALE*

I won't take my religion from any man who never
works except with his mouth and never cherishes any
memory except the face of the woman on the American
silver dollar.

— CARL SANDBURG, FROM *TO A CONTEMPORARY BUNKSHOOTER*

To many pastors and professors from my generation, the
book deal is the ultimate status symbol. We're too savvy to
admit publicly that we find status in our cars or our homes or
the size of our bank accounts, as these are so clearly "worldly"
affections and idols. We would even, I think, deny that con-
gregational size matters, deft as we are at telling ourselves and
others that it's not numbers that concern us.

But the book deal. Ahhh . . . the book deal. The dream of ripping open that large United Parcel Service (UPS) delivery with *Crossway* or *Moody* or *Thomas Nelson* written on the box, our wives gazing on adoringly from the background. The affirmation from outside that our ideas matter. The glory of pulling out that first copy, seeing our name on the cover, and then smelling that intoxicating combination of printer's ink, paper, and binding. And, finally, the thrill of snapping a photo of said open box, and then posting it on Twitter or Facebook, because in our generation nothing has really happened unless it has been photographed, archived, congratulated, and commented upon via social media. In an episode of *Seinfeld*, one of Jerry's friends said, "You've gotta see the *baby*." My generation demands that we gaze adoringly at each other's books.[1]

The book, today, is what makes us special. It's what makes us "not just another pastor" or "not just another college professor." Academia has forever openly used and celebrated the book as a rung on the ladder to success, and now, it seems, many in the church are doing the same thing. When we're talking to others about our church, we make qualifying statements like, "I mean, the pastor's not *famous* or anything, but he's still really good." What we're really saying is, "Although the publishing industry and the evangelical fan base aren't currently aware of my pastor, I still think he's really great." We shouldn't have to make that statement.

Even the stairway to publishing heaven is fraught with dilemma. The Gospel Coalition website is your classic mixed blessing. On one hand it's the sort of de facto online gathering place for New Calvinism, with all of the good and bad that entails. It's a place for thought-provoking articles and commentary written primarily by pastors and for pastors who are part of the movement and who have a real love for the gospel and the Word of God. The editorial staff works hard to acquire quality articles and curtail the kind of nastiness that tends to happen online. It's also a place where some much-needed vetting of churches happens, such that when a person is moving to a new community he or she can find a church that is in some way a part of the TGC orbit.

It's also become a place to promote your book, to get articles published so that you can get a book deal to promote, and to follow and comment on those pastors and personalities who are already famous enough to have articles published and get commented upon.[2] There's a semi-addictive quality to the TGC blogs, much like Facebook and Twitter, such that not checking comes with the niggling feeling that you may be missing out on something, but checking and reading a few articles and comments almost always has the opposite of an encouraging effect on me. I'm almost always discouraged by either the hero worship or the viciousness with which commenters go after one another online.[3]

I'm almost always left with the feeling that we'd all be better off without the blog and always end up even more intrigued by the pastors I respect who don't seem to "need" this kind of fame and promotion, such as Tim Keller and John Piper. That said, nearly every pastor I know wants to get an article published on the TGC website. Incidentally, I'm regularly checking TGC because I'm waiting for them to post an article that I've written. Full disclosure. I'm not above the TGC obsession.

"The book," of course, isn't just a book. The book is the conduit to the speaking gig, which may be, after a number of years, the conduit to the podcast, which is the conduit to the radio show. All of this may be the conduit to bookings on evangelical cruises, where Christians pay to sail to exotic ports of call with famous pastor/authors. The fact that I just typed that last sentence and it's not a joke makes me a little queasy.[4]

There may be no bigger thrill for today's pastor than to add his *own* title to the book table in the narthex. For those of us who have been published, there's even the thrill of being able to open doors for others and make *their* dreams come true. We feel like big shots, sharing names of editors and making things happen for our friends. At the end of the day, this serves the ultimate purpose of making us feel awesome about ourselves.

IS CHRIST ALONE ENOUGH?

I should point out that a great many books do a great deal of good for a great number of people. I can name a handful of them myself, books that I can thank God for because they help me to know Him more and to love Him better.

The question then is, how much of what I have been describing is *wrong* or *sin*? I've done most of these things (minus, of course, the cruises). I'm not a pastor, but I was thrilled to see my books on the book table at my church. I've taken the Facebook photo of my new book and posted it and then trolled for comments. I've even gotten buzzed on opening publishing doors for my friends. The question, sinwise, is "Do I *need* to be published?" Do I need a book deal to feel like a legitimate pastor or, for me, to feel like I'm succeeding at not being ordinary? Or is Christ, alone, enough?

At the beginning of my writing career, and at times since, writing was a legitimate artistic outlet. I had a passion to communicate well and be understood. Sometimes it's been a stroke to my ego and a way to avoid being ordinary, although, ironically, it seems like everyone I know has a book deal now.

It should be noted that there is a law of diminishing returns at play in each of those scenarios. It's less thrilling to see my books today than it was in 2006 when *Facing Tyson* came out and Kristin and I made a special trip to the bookstore[5] just to see it.[6] Today there's a sobriety to the process, the realization that outside of an act of God, my books probably won't be *New York Times* bestsellers. The boxes sit, unopened, as no one rushes into the office to see me rip open the UPS box. What was once a thrill for everyone has become a little bit commonplace. For Kristin, the next book deal is a few more months of being able to buy groceries and make mortgage payments. For my kids, a book deal may mean a little nicer Christmas or an Xbox. In this, getting published is a crass, utilitarian pursuit. It's the opposite of art.

TRUE SPIRITUAL GREATNESS

Perhaps Christ wants me to feel like less of an artist and be less celebrated. Perhaps He's demanding that my writing be less of an ego trip.

He may be calling you to something similar. He may be asking you to be less obsessive and driven about getting the book deal—or whatever it is that you think will validate you as a pastor or a professor or a writer. He may be calling you out of fame, or at least out of the dream of fame.

We see this tension between worldly ambition and godly ambition in our publishing pursuits, but we also see it in Matthew 20, where there is some serious family-related fame maneuvering taking place. In verse 21, the mother of James and John approaches Jesus and asks, "Grant that one of these two sons of mine may sit at your right and the other at your left in your kingdom." Her sons, no doubt, implored her to make this request, which was aimed at elevating their fame above that of the other ten.

As parents we can relate to this all too well—a desire for our own fame, and a desire to be known through the achievements of our children. On one hand (positive), she had a rock-solid belief that Jesus would be ushering in the kingdom. She had no doubt on that point. On the other hand (negative), she wanted her sons to be co-vice presidents in the new venture.

Jesus puts her request into context, telling the two men, "You don't know what you are asking. Can you drink the cup I am going to drink?" (v. 22). James and John replied in the affirmative, and they would both, indeed, suffer in their own lives, as James was the first of the twelve to die for his Lord, beheaded by Herod Agrippa I, and John was the last, suffering exile to the Island of Patmos. Their stories suggest that suffering and true identification with Jesus are inextricably linked. It may be impossible to have one without the other.

Jesus then explains that the privilege of sitting at His right and left "is not for me to grant" (v. 23). Not surprisingly, when the other ten heard of this request, the text says that "they were indignant with the two brothers" (v. 24). When fame is reached for, and even at some level attained, jealousy and strife often follow. I've seen this in my own life and career. Publishing has been a great blessing to me—and also, at times, something of a curse. It's launched some friendships and wrecked others. Go into it with your eyes open and your heart guarded. It probably won't be what you want it to be, and if it is, that might be worse.

Interestingly, Jesus doesn't say that we shouldn't be great. He doesn't implore James and John to just shoot for mediocrity. Rather, He closes the issue with a meditation on the *true* nature of greatness in verses 25-28, saying:

> *You know that the rulers of the Gentiles lord it over them, and their high officials exercise authority over them. Not so with you. Instead, whoever wants to become great among you must be your servant, and whoever wants to be first must be your slave—just as the Son of Man did not come to be served, but to serve, and to give his life as a ransom for many.*

SERVING OR BEING SERVED?

Fame in general (evangelical or otherwise) is mostly about being served. The conference circuit is nice because it's generally populated with people who (a) think you're awesome, and (b) don't want anything from you other than a signed book and maybe a photo for their Facebook page. But we learn in Matthew that for God to call you "great," you must endeavor to serve others. Family, as we'll discuss in more detail in the next chapter, is nothing if not an opportunity to humbly serve. Every backpack full of homework, every sick child, every evening lost to baseball practice, and even every long seemingly fruitless conversation with a difficult family member, can be an opportunity to serve.

I'm convicted by the idea that God sees what we human beings can't, and that in eternity a great many who followed Him without fame or acclaim will be exalted. I'm convicted by the idea that we're not called to seek fame or influence, but rather to take up our cross and follow Christ.

Ultimately, it's a question of motives. Do I want to be published to serve others—or to serve myself? Is my attitude—especially as I progress in my career—one of entitlement or one of humble service, even in a field that our culture celebrates?

⇒ *From Kristin* ⇐

Everybody wants to do something lasting, make some long-term mark on the world. Many people think of writing as the way to do this. It's a way to record an actual part of yourself that could, theoretically, live forever, could potentially influence people, even lots of people, and could change the world. Becoming famous—even just a little famous in a little niche market like the Christian retail market—is another real draw. But even if you can't be an author, or become semifamous, to brush shoulders with someone who has is nearly as good.

So I am married to someone who has made a meaningful and possibly long-term contribution to literature and who has a little sheen of "fame." And there seems to be a long list of people who want to meet, talk to, hang out with him because of this. Sometimes this is a good thing. Ted can encourage (and be encouraged by) a stimulating assortment of people. We have a broad and intriguing list of people (some famous themselves, but most not) whom we've connected with. I love the aspect of our life that takes us lots of different places and gives us the chance to interact with new people. The exchange of ideas that has been generated has contributed greatly to my growth as a person—intellectually, emotionally, spiritually, culturally. But it can be negative too; people want to use Ted to get their own stuff going or to add another "famous acquaintance" story to their dossier. Some people want to have a person to put on a pedestal; this is very dangerous for them, but also for Ted. Being on a pedestal, being worshipped (even if no one would call it that outright) is heady, addictive stuff. For someone like Ted, whose besetting sin is being a people pleaser, being everyone's hero is a dangerous elixir. The more adoration he gets, the more he wants. Jealousy when he sees others getting it, especially when he "needs" another hit of adoration, can be all-consuming.

And then there is my sin. It's funny, when we met, I was the outgoing, chatty extrovert, and Ted was the quieter introvert. I had to twist his arm to convince him we should invite another couple over for dinner with us. In fact, these characterizations are still largely true (although I no longer have to sweet-talk Ted into having company; dinners with friends have become a near necessity for us). Yet Ted is the one who constantly gets calls, texts, e-mails, and invites while I have my few faithful friends. I get to tag along to many of his interactions, but it has sometimes been a source of frustration (read: conflict) for me when I feel like he's got so much going on and I, well, don't. It hurts my pride, and it reveals my own idol of wanting to be popular, well-liked, constantly surrounded by a passel of people who like me for me—not for being married to Ted.

At the same time, there is my own pride by association. Even though I sometimes resent all the attention Ted gets, I am also happy to bask in the reflected glow. I am ashamed to admit this, but I have been known to speak just a little louder when discussing "my husband's current book manuscript/agent/writing seminar" in hopes that someone will overhear and think I'm even more awesome (than they already thought just based on my cool-hippy-arty look—oops, another idol!) by association. Ted and I took a night to celebrate the contract for this very book—my first actual opportunity to wear the Writer Hat myself—and as we were sitting in the restaurant, reading and signing the contract, I showed it to the waiter. Ridiculous! But I did. At various points in our life, finances have necessitated me having a job, which also attacks our idols of Having the Perfect Reformed Family, where the husband makes so much money and the wife is such a good financial manager that she never has to work outside of the home. Not a bad thing to shoot for, but it hasn't always worked this way for us.

One of the jobs I've had has been cleaning a church (read: janitor. Pretty humbling). And at this church I clean, there is a big bookshelf that displays all the books for sale, many by the church's pastor and staff. Included on this table are a couple of books coauthored by my husband. One of my duties has been to dust this shelf weekly. The irony of being paid a lowly wage to clean the shelf that houses my husband's books is never lost on me. Yet I still have wanted to shout out to people passing by, "Hey, I may look like a humble janitor, but see this book I'm dusting? My husband wrote it. So I'm not, actually, just a janitor. Just thought you should know that." I'm not even sure how you would classify that idol—pride? Recognition? Thinking I'm above the station God has allowed me to occupy?—but there it is.

In the church, the book is the equivalent of the red Corvette (without seeming as materialistic and shallow). It's the status symbol we all want but rarely talk about wanting. The publishing idol doesn't just affect the author, but also those in the author's orbit.

CHAPTER 11

A Chance to Lose Your Life

WHAT FAMILY SHOWCASES

Whoever loses their life for me will find it.
— MATTHEW 16:25

My mother-in-law shuffles nervously into my office after dropping off my kids. Almost every time we see each other lately, she asks about this book in such a way as to try to mask her nervousness, but what she may really be asking is this: "Into how much detail are you going to go about our family's brokenness?" In other words, how much spilling of the proverbial beans are you going to do, and how might it impact or not impact our collective reputations?

What I don't tell her is that I've agonized over this very question. And, for now, the answer is, "I don't know." What I do tell her is that it's a book about household gods, to which she replies, "That sounds interesting." To which I reply, "It will be interesting, I think." Semi-awkward silence ensues.

Her unwillingness to venture a follow-up question and my unwillingness to volunteer any additional information about the book speak volumes. She asks because she loves us, and she cares. Though I open up some veins in this book, there are others I don't open, because I care for her as well. I should just tell her that. I don't know why it's so hard.

If we were the kind of people who came right out and said things, she would ask, "How much are you going to say about me-slash-our-family in the book?" and I would have a ready answer. Family and relationships are complex and difficult. For curiosity-assuaging purposes, suffice it to say that our family brokenness is both worse than you could ever imagine and also, by the grace of God alone, not all that terrible at this point. It's only because of Christ that both things can be true. If you know Jesus, and have a family, you can probably relate to this at some level.

What's scary (to her and to me) about a book like this is that it does threaten our carefully crafted and usually subconscious veneer of perfection. We want people to think our families are healthy and happy. And saying or writing anything otherwise is, at some level, a life-losing proposition. I would argue that being part of a family is a chance to lose your life.

LOSING YOUR LIFE

Family, simply stated, is an opportunity to lose your life, because being part of a family means subjugating your desires to others. Things cannot and will not always be the way you want them to be. The moment you enter into a family—be it through marriage, through child rearing, or even through being a child or a sibling, you lose a part of your life.

Parents feel this acutely. Most days my desire to have a quiet morning is crucified to the reality that I live in a house with two small boys. I wake up every morning to the sound of their loud, rambunctious play. I often lie in bed annoyed and think, *Why couldn't they be quiet and considerate* once *in a while?* or *Why does their play always include thumping, banging, screeching, and loud laughter?* In this scenario, losing my life for His sake may mean lying in bed and choosing to thank God for the sound of two happy, healthy boys playing together. Thanking God for the fact that despite my sins and imperfections, I still have a wife who loves me and two healthy, rowdy, life-loving little boys under my care.

Sometimes family gives us an opportunity to lose our lives in deeper, more permanent ways. Sometimes losing our lives means caring for an elderly parent who has lost his or her mind. Anybody who has taken the lonely, dark walks into nursing homes and care facilities with loved ones knows how challenging this can be. There's a sense of finality and hopelessness within those walls. Visiting a parent with Alzheimer's or dementia can feel agonizing, and tears almost always follow.

Sometimes losing our lives means loving a child or a spouse who doesn't love us back. Sometimes it means losing the dream of the perfect marriage or having to face the pain of an apostate child. Sometimes losing our lives comes in the loss of face and status that follows acknowledging our sin before others and humbly asking their forgiveness.

In all of these scenarios, God can be glorified, which, if you think about it, is the incongruous, audacious part of the gospel. God is glorified when we apologize to our spouses and kids for sins great and small. God is glorified when they forgive us. Both of these things, to the world, don't often make sense. Only God can take something that was meant for evil (sin) and use it for good.

A SHOWCASE FOR REPENTANCE

There is perhaps nothing more like losing your life, in the Matthew 16:25 sense,[1] than acknowledging your sin before others, especially others in your family who may admire you, revere you, or even worship you.

First John 1:9 reads, "If we confess our sins, he is faithful and just and will forgive us our sins and purify us from all unrighteousness." This is a scriptural promise we can cling to. Oftentimes we want the Bible to say, "God will help us pay our mortgage," or "He'll give us perfect kids," but the reality is that we *can* count on this promise. If we confess, with a humble and contrite heart, God *will* lift the burden and darkness of guilt.

I've done this. I've confessed my sins to my wife and children with fear and trembling, but at the behest of the Holy Spirit. It *is* painful, but I've seen God glorified through my obedience and have had those relationships deepened and restored in ways I would have thought, in my flesh, were impossible.

If you're married, I invite you to confess your household gods—the need to win, the idolatry of money and things, the need to impress others—to your spouse and ask for prayer. You can, and should, involve your church. Pastors are dying to see hearts changed by the gospel in their congregations, and yours would love to pray with you about these issues and pressures.

If you've hurt members of your family—your spouse, your kids, your parents—and are feeling the conviction of the Spirit, confess. Articulate the exact nature of your wrongs and avoid generalities such as "I made a mistake." God will honor your courage to call a sin a sin. The relationship may feel broken for a while. You may feel moments of great fear. But in God's economy, when we confess, the sin is removed by the power of the Cross, "As far as the east is from the west."[2] And as Paul writes powerfully in Romans 8:1, there is "now no condemnation for those who are in Christ Jesus."

A SHOWCASE FOR FORGIVENESS

Being part of a family—being married, being a parent, being a son or a daughter—gives us an opportunity to forgive and, therefore, be more like Christ. We forgive because Christ forgave. If you're part of a family, chances are you've been wronged. You've at least been ignored or had your feelings disregarded, or perhaps you've been hurt deeply by abuse or adultery. When we forgive, God is glorified, and His greatness is magnified.

Forgiveness, to the world, is madness. Revenge, "getting

yours," and "quitting with dignity intact" are all worldly values. Forgiving when you've been hurt is, as the Bible says,
"foolishness to those who are perishing."[3]

Matthew 18:23-35 shows a picture of the forgiveness that
we're supposed to extend, because we ourselves have been
forgiven. In this account we're shown a man who owes his
king "ten thousand bags of gold," which, in today's economy,
would amount to over six billion dollars. After some serious begging and pleading, the king takes pity on the man
and cancels his debt. This man, who should have been filled
with thankfulness and gratitude, instead goes and finds a guy
who owes him a hundred silver coins, grabs him, and starts
to choke him. In a perfect twist of irony, this guy begs for
mercy, and rather than extending the same sort of forgiveness
and gratitude, he refuses and has the guy thrown into prison.

The king gets wind of the man's unwillingness to forgive,
and has him jailed and tortured until he's able to pay back
his original debt (which we can only assume will be never).
Verse 35 is a chilling end to the story, and underscores how
important forgiveness is to God: "This is how my heavenly
Father will treat each of you unless you forgive your brother
or sister from your heart."

Family is nothing if not a place to offer forgiveness. And
we are not to forgive as the world does, with hearts of bitterness and revenge fantasies. We're to forgive as Christ forgave.
What this looks like, practically, often involves refusing to
stand on our own rights, and even, at times, disregarding our
own feelings. It involves refusing to take revenge, even when

taking revenge seems like the greatest thing in the world. It involves genuinely extending kindness to the person who wronged us, even when it doesn't feel right to do so.

We're also blessed, tangibly, when we forgive. Our hearts are cleansed of bitterness and malice when we allow others to repent, and when we forgive. It is in forgiving that we become most like Christ. That doesn't mean that the forgiveness is always easy or clean, and it doesn't mean that the relationships immediately go back to the way they looked before.

PROOF THAT WE NEED CHRIST

I need Christ always, but I especially need Him in February, in Michigan. February in Michigan is brutal. Any and all "charm" that comes with winter and snow is gone, replaced by day after day of snow, bad roads, clouds, and, for me, some dark hopelessness. Every year I say things like, "We have to get out of here," and yet, here we are.

I'm not a hero to my wife. I'm not her knight in shining armor. Nor am I the perfect dad for my sons. I'm not a football hero or even a tenured professor. But yet, in Christ, my family still loves me. And our love for one another is still growing, still evolving. This gives me hope.

Psalm 73:25-26 reads, "Whom have I in heaven but you? And earth has nothing I desire besides you. My flesh and my heart may fail, but God is the strength of my heart and my portion forever." Winter, and family, both remind me that God *must* be the strength of my heart and my portion forever. I can't survive life or generate happiness on the strength of my own dreams and ambitions. I can't be a good enough, let alone perfect, husband and father.

God uses our families, large or small, to sanctify us. He brings challenges into our lives that we might never face if we lived apart from family. My two kids are two people who stretch my patience, but I'm called to love them and not exasperate them. I'm called to love my wife as Christ loved His church. I can't do either of these things without Christ. I lean on God because I have to, but also because His goodness is so compelling.

He gives the forgiving embrace of a wife who's been hurt, but who chooses to love me anyway because He gives her the grace to do so. He gives little graces . . . the smell of Maxim's clean hair after a bath, an afternoon spent shooting baskets in the basement with the boys, a new video game to enjoy together, *Brady Bunch* reruns on TV, a workout with my dad. He moves someone I've hurt to send me a letter of reconciliation, which is yet more proof that He is real. He gives us the next breath. He gives us the gift of each other.

And for these things, I'm thankful.

Endnotes

ACKNOWLEDGMENTS
1. This always struck me as an interesting and particularly subtext-heavy way to refer to a certain kind of family unit.

AUTHOR'S NOTE
1. *The Royal Tenenbaums, The Life Aquatic, Bottle Rocket*
2. *The Life Aquatic, Fantastic Mr. Fox, The Royal Tenenbaums, Rushmore*
3. *The Royal Tenenbaums, The Life Aquatic, Rushmore*
4. Probably all of them
5. *Fantastic Mr. Fox, The Royal Tenenbaums, Moonrise Kingdom*
6. Richie Tenenbaum, Whack Bat
7. *The Life Aquatic, The Royal Tenenbaums*
8. All of them
9. All of them except *Fantastic Mr. Fox*

INTRODUCTION: FAMILY IDOLATRY AND OTHER HOUSEHOLD GODS
1. The best refrigerator-ready Christmas card I ever saw was from R. C. Sproul. He was seated in a regal, high-backed chair (a throne?), resplendent in a suit, with his wife at his elbow and a huge, menacing-looking German shepherd at his feet and a fireplace in the background. It looked like the kind of Christmas card you publish if you've just conquered and annexed a small country.
2. Timothy Keller, *Counterfeit Gods* (New York: Dutton, 2009), xvii.
3. Keller, xvii.
4. Proverbs 12:4; 31
5. Psalm 127:3-5

6. 1 Timothy 3:4-5,12; Titus 2:3-5; Ephesians 5:21-33; 6:1-4
7. Thank you, Cory Hartman, for this quote . . . or for the conversation that led to this quote.

CHAPTER 1: SPAWNING FAMILY IDOLATRY

1. This is verbatim.
2. Genesis 1:28, KJV
3. Matthew 5:15
4. A. W. Tozer, *The Pursuit of God* (Camp Hill, PA: Christian Publications, Inc., 1982), 93.
5. Janet Fishburn, *Confronting the Idolatry of Family* (Nashville, TN: Abingdon Press, 1991), 26.
6. Nowadays, parents often show their kids off in Christmas cards and Facebook postings.
7. The actual copy promoting these things sounds so much like something satirical that I would write *about* these things that I realize I couldn't write it any funnier than it actually *is*.
8. But how awesome would it have been if he had?
9. Which will probably always keep us relatively unsuccessful. Thank you, 1990s.
10. Romans 3:9
11. Romans 3:10
12. Romans 3:23
13. Not that this is always family idolatry. But really? Fifth grade?
14. Ephesians 2:1

CHAPTER 2: LOVE WILL TEAR YOU APART

1. Via elaborate and lengthy infant baptism ceremonies
2. The rest of the time, in general
3. Janet Fishburn, *Confronting the Idolatry of Family* (Nashville, TN: Abingdon Press, 1991), 21.
4. 1 Corinthians 7:32-33
5. A version of this content originally appeared at www.gospelcoalition.org.
6. If I could "be" anyone from a movie, it would probably be Dr. Jules Hilbert from *Stranger Than Fiction.*
7. I think Timothy Keller came up with this phrase, but I'm not sure. It sounds like the kind of thing he would come up with.
8. Genesis 29:9-18
9. Genesis 29:19-21
10. Genesis 29:22-24

11. Genesis 29:25-30
12. Genesis 29:31-32
13. Alternate names: Town Location, Hamlet Spot
14. All of which came with the question (from me), "Is there a cash award?" and the disappointing reality that awards are great but you can't use them to pay bills.
15. Getting a job and going to work
16. James 1:2-4

CHAPTER 3: YOU SHOULD BE SO PROUD
1. Genesis 15:1-3
2. Genesis 15:4-6
3. Genesis 16:1-2
4. Genesis 16:2-5
5. Genesis 17:15-18
6. Genesis 17:19-22
7. Genesis 22:15-18

CHAPTER 4: BLUE CHIPS
1. H. G. Bissinger, *Friday Night Lights* (New York: Addison Wesley, 1990), 109.
2. 1 John 5:21

CHAPTER 5: ON WRITING AND GRINDING CONCRETE
1. Gut Check Press. www.gutcheckpress.com.
2. Thanks to my friends Cory and Kelly Hartman, I am the proud ironic owner of a Joel Osteen board game called "Your Best Life Now."
3. *The Heidelberg Catechism* (Grand Rapids, MI: Faith Alive Christian Resources, 1988), 9.

CHAPTER 6: BE PERFECT
1. Don DeLillo, *Underworld* (New York: Scribner, 1997), 715.
2. A.W. Tozer, *The Pursuit of God* (Camp Hill, PA: Christian Publications, Inc., 1982), 45.
3. Cheryl Forbes, *The Religion of Power* (Grand Rapids, MI: Zondervan, 1983), 35.
4. Like the wan, pale, passive-looking, rouge-cheeked, semicreepy, eighties bearded Jesus in the painting in your grandparents' Baptist church. Look for this next time you go to church with them. . . . It's there. I promise.
5. This is the one in which Rocky watches his friend Apollo die in the ring, comes out of retirement, flies to Siberia to train, runs up the side of a

mountain, avenges Apollo's death by beating the steroid-addled Drago, and then finally grabs a microphone from the announcer and gives a passionate speech that is applauded by all the Russians in attendance who previously hated him. Also, he ends the Cold War. *Rocky IV* may be the best bad movie ever made.

CHAPTER 7: HEROD'S TEMPLE

1. As to what this means, your guess is as good as mine. . . .
2. Some of this originally appeared at www.tedkluck.com.
3. Cheryl Forbes, *The Religion of Power* (Grand Rapids, MI: Zondervan, 1983), 64.

CHAPTER 8: DOES GOD LOVE ME OR IS HE A COSMIC TRICKSTER?

1. Seriously, this couldn't be made up.
2. Kristin and I are both artists, and we have, between us, zero ability to plan for or manage our personal finances. The fact that we're still afloat after seventeen years of marriage is nothing short of a miracle.
3. Psalm 27:13

CHAPTER 9: LOVE ME, LOVE ME, SAY THAT YOU LOVE ME

1. Be fruitful and multiply.
2. Originally appeared at www.tedkluck.com
3. If you're not the kind of Christian who feels called to be photographed with needy third-world children and then called to repost those photographs, I question whether you're a Christian at all.
4. I'll take the liberty, at this point, of preemptively writing the one-star reviews that will come as a result of this section that go something like this: "I love Facebook and use it to keep in touch with my missionary friends who live overseas and my aunt [insert name] who is homebound and who can't communicate any other way. I think it's judgmental of you to assume that I'm using Facebook just to feed my own ego." Feel free to copy and paste that directly into the Amazon.com review section.
5. The other one-star review that I'll get goes something like this—again feel free to directly copy and paste: "I'm a pastor and I use social media to stay connected to my congregants, sharing things like sermons and Scripture to encourage them on a daily basis. I'm offended that you would suggest that I'm doing this just for my own benefit. Social media is a legitimate part of my ministry and workday."
6. See: clichés, evangelical.
7. Ibid.

8. I have an antiquated website (www.tedkluck.com) and a Facebook "author" page that somebody else maintains for me.
9. There will be a special place in hell for whoever invented this number.
10. In certain sub-subcultures of our church, I feel like Dave Ramsey ranks just beneath the Holy Trinity in terms of magnitude and reputation. Somewhere Dave Ramsey is lighting a cigar with a hundred dollar bill and laughing his way to the bank.

CHAPTER 10: YOU'VE GOTTA SEE MY BOOK
1. And still, it should be noted, demands that we gaze at each other's actual babies, of which there are many.
2. In this way it's not unlike the late EmergentVillage.com (rest its soul), which I suspect eventually collapsed under the weight of its own celebrity culture and self-importance. Also, I think people got tired of reading different versions of the same three articles. I'd hate to see the same thing happen to GospelCoalition, but I'd also kind of like to see the same thing happen to GospelCoalition.
3. Whenever I write an article there, I'm always discouraged by the same things.
4. That being said, I would take one of these bookings in a heartbeat. My punk-rock sensibilities only go so far.
5. Rest their souls.
6. Incidentally, when we were there in 2006 we ran into a friend of my mother-in-law who made much of the book (even though it was about boxing), went to the effort of getting me to sign the book in her presence, went to the effort of making us think she was going to buy it, and then put it back on the shelf. I know this because a friend of mine bought the copy the next day, brought it over, and said, "But it looks like somebody has already scribbled in the front of it." He was referring to my signature. It feels good to tell that story.

CHAPTER 11: A CHANCE TO LOSE YOUR LIFE
1. "Whoever loses their life for me will find it."
2. Psalm 103:12
3. 1 Corinthians 1:18